Sex, Drugs and Techno

A Journey to the Brink - and Beyond

Sex, Drugs and Techno

A Journey to the Brink - and Beyond

Paul Eldridge

BOOKS

Winchester, UK
Washington, USA

First published by O-Books, 2011
O-Books is an imprint of John Hunt Publishing Ltd., Laurel House, Station Approach,
Alresford, Hants, SO24 9JH, UK
office1@o-books.net
www.o-books.com

For distributor details and how to order please visit the 'Ordering' section on our website.

Text copyright: Paul Eldridge 2010

ISBN: 978 1 84694 511 3

A CIP catalogue record for this book is available from the British Library.

Design: Tom Davies

Printed in the UK by CPI Antony Rowe
Printed in the USA by Offset Paperback Mfrs, Inc

We operate a distinctive and ethical publishing philosophy in all
areas of our business, from our global network of authors to
production and worldwide distribution.

CONTENTS

Om Swastiastu Ratu Bagus

Introduction*

THE WESTERN WORLD PARTIES with no borders or boundaries. We all share similar social experiences of music, fashion,
attractions and interactive habits. What I engage in on Saturday
night can be ventured in every Western city on the planet by like-
minded people aged from about eighteen to forty-plus and the
scattered party veterans who look like they haven't stopped since
the '60s. This global scene is all about drinking, socialising,
music, the opposite sex, the same sex — and drugs. All one needs
to be part of this global community is a sense of fun and daring
nocturnal adventure.

This book is about what I have experienced, felt, discovered
and healed, living the way of my generation by way of the
influence of partying and drugs. If you have just begun to
explore the world of social freedom and experimentation, it
shows you what the party scene may have in store for you if you
stay on the circuit. For those who have been there, done that,
here lies an exposition to help you understand exactly what the
mystery of drugs has done — and possibly is continuing to do —
to you.

Drugs and partying are so entrenched in our society and such
an easy trap to fall into, again and again. Experiencing drugs
opens a palatable gateway into the unknown, which can start off
quite liberating, only to lead down the same sorry path,
countless times fatally. Though what exactly *is* taking place on
this journey and its destination? I was led to believe that it's
simply an ingested chemical charge that releases my body's own
chemicals — that elevates me to bliss and then depletes 'this' and
'that', making me shitty, depressed and at times suicidal. But
there is a bigger picture as to why drugs begin with pleasure and
end in pain, and it has taken me an incredible journey to uncover
the stark reality behind this mystery that plays through drug-

induced tantalised senses, in a 'game' that has been known to wise people for thousands of years. It is a game the doctors never mention.

The allure is too great. The social scene continually entices the like-minded to 'taste' that sublime altered state, while community service warnings alarm us of the dangers and government policy bases itself around a greater police effort to *try* and inhibit the flow of drugs onto the streets, which bears no results. Drugs are out there in society and are accessible to anyone who wants them — any place, any time. And there are plenty of takers.

Everything has a price, and the hardened dance party (or rave) revolutionaries know only too well the price we can pay for pushing partying to its limits. To the newcomers, I honestly can't tell you, 'Don't take drugs', as no matter how strongly I now oppose them or no matter what you are warned or told, we know life doesn't work that way. You will always want to experience first hand, regardless of what I, parents or the government present to you. With this book you will at least have a bit of credence and forewarning, showing you what to expect, what it all means and how to overcome that potential bump on the path. For many of the tormented lost souls travelling aimlessly day to day at the end of the ride, the only avenue available to rehabilitate is a doctor waiting to prescribe more chemicals.

To parents and those concerned with the plight of drugs, the information here is exactly the type of help I was once in desperate need of. I could find limited plausible guidance and reference material, especially when drugs were taking their strongest, most destructive, grip on my life. I did not understand the bizarre world they exposed me to. Finding someone who *really* understood the consequences of the way I lived and played, showing empathy and believing my outlandish experiences was far from easy. Continually reading that ecstasy depletes serotonin

— *That's why I'm feeling so shitty* — didn't go far enough for me. I needed cutting-edge answers to the expansive *truth* within the powerful cycle of drugs. Plus, I tired of buying self-help books by life gurus with million-dollar smiles living in Tinsel Town, with many proclaiming that healing and wellness are such easy and carefree states of achieving and being. Nothing personal against them, but for some reason — I eventually understood why — I felt self-help books never really helped me get to the ultimate source of my experiences and suffering from drugs.

A drug-induced life can't be cured in the time it takes you to read this book, or any book proclaiming the words, 'Wow. That's it. I get it!' It takes hard work beyond the confines of the mind and body. It takes soul searching. It's not overcome with a detox program. It's an ongoing journey of discovery about the many layers and 'masks' of oneself and the dynamics of the world around us, initially littered with a few highs and many lows. It's a huge test that must be passed. It depends on how much you want to discover the real you. I believed once that I discovered the real me with drugs. But, as time passed, the real me seemed like a fantasy for another life.

What gives me the right to present this book, setting myself up as an expert on the highs and lows of drugs and the party scene? I'm not a doctor, a psychiatrist or a counsellor. While I cannot lay claim to any medical certificate hanging from my wall, I can share with you more than twenty-five years of knowledge about the topic from a powerful position of first-hand experience and hard-earned understanding. It was an insatiable quest in discovering — in the wrong and right way — myself and the world around me that could never be learnt in a classroom or a clinic. That experience and understanding was like a PhD, with the topic and attainment being life itself.

I've helped create the mind-altering experiences that cliquishly have drawn many to in-vogue clubs and stadiums to get totally wasted. A former international DJ, I mixed the musical pulse that turned music into a cathartic journey. I created a transcendent platform for crowds through DJing and also shared the journey· as a face in the crowd on the dance floor — in numerous states of altered mind.

In the course of growing up and as an adult I have had many challenging and powerful experiences. These were valuable lessons to take heed of, but I showed a total disregard for many things moral or safe, not to mention legal. Sadly, other friends of mine who shared similar experiences never got a chance to amend their past. I did. My second chance allowed me to embark upon a new course, a new learning experience, which presented me with the opportunity to truly understand the most important and challenging topic of them all — my life.

I've not known of, nor heard about, a drug lifestyle leading to a healthy and happy life. Drugs are not designed to provide such gifts. Incredibly, my life was spared the demise experienced by so many drug users. Why? Well, I don't know, I am not some sort of self-ordained individual who professes to be living an enlightened life.

The reason you are reading this book is because I was fortunate enough to meet some incredible people who somehow entered my life right on cue. At crucial moments they appeared and provided me with incredible guidance, lifting the veil on my mysterious experiences and my past. Their unorthodox method-ologies helped me to understand what it was I was trying to uncover and paved the way not only for me to heal, but also to open my eyes to the world around me and open my heart — naturally. This book is the story of that journey.

This book exposes the social drug scene as it really was — and still is. Some may find parts of my story overwhelming, but it's the way an entire generation has expressed themselves without regard. What I did, so too did many others. Countless sons and daughters, brothers and sisters, neighbours and friends, are living this life right now, with no idea where it is taking them.

What I spent years experiencing, searching for and discovering, I share here with you.

---

* All the events described in this book are factual. The names of most individuals mentioned have been changed to protect their privacy.

Part One

1. The opening curtain

MY FAST-LANE JOURNEY took shape way back when I was a teen in the '80s and during some of life's toughest challenges well before that. Home was the Sydney beachside suburb of Maroubra. Its local surfers were renowned for going hard. Today, they are known as the Bra Boys. Back then, we didn't have the much-publicised reputation the Bra Boys have now, but not too much has changed. Surfing, partying, fighting — you either kept up the pace, and the standard, or you burnt out and faded into obscurity. Many paid for this intense lifestyle with their lives, in all manner of fashion. It was an early exit from a lifestyle we honoured and cherished.

The only boy, with one younger sister and two older sisters, we seemed a normal suburban family, living in a nice little rented house in Maroubra's adjoining suburb, Coogee. Mum, tall and blonde, epitomised the beach girl image of her hometown of Bondi beach. Dad, dark in complexion and about half a foot shorter than Mum, was from the country town of Goulburn, and carried that typical Australian bush trait of seeing the funny, and sarcastic, side to everything. Dad spent fourteen years in the navy, and my parents' affinity with the ocean certainly rubbed off on me. With my sheet white hair that sat on my shoulders and big blue eyes, I was a typical little beach 'grommet', as beach kids are affectionately known. Mum cooked beautiful meals every night and made sure we always looked neat and tidy. We were disciplined the old-fashioned way when we got out of hand — mostly by Mum — and attended the local Catholic schools. Mum and Dad were never into getting excited about dreams. They thought it far preferable to have a stable job packing shelves at the supermarket than pursue frivolous entrepreneurial dreams. I had many dreams, but I learnt it was better to keep them to myself.

I was a bit of a larrikin at school, which often seemed to land me at the vice-principal's office for four of the best. I never really understood how those patrons of Jesus, all loving and compassionate, could suddenly turn into sadists, caning us in a frenzy for acts such as simply laughing in church.

While us kids received the utmost care and attention, we lived with a dark secret. Mum worked at a club on the other side of the harbour and I remember sitting up with Dad on the weekends watching John Wayne movies and the like and listening to Dad's navy stories while Mum was at work. But I always feared going to bed because I knew terrible things were certain to happen. From my earliest memories, I recall the countless times of waking and standing behind the lounge room door, hiding, as my parents argued to that point I knew was always coming. Bang! Crash!

I stood at that door, enduring long and vicious arguments, because I knew that, when the moment arrived, I could be there in an instant — in between Mum and Dad as they punched into one another like a couple of street fighters, both full of Scotch whisky. Crying and screaming in sheer terror for them to stop, I couldn't understand how they could do that to each other. I couldn't understand how they could do that to us... again and again. Both of them were as much to blame as the other. The smell of Scotch whisky was a constant reminder. That smell meant trouble was looming and, even today, the aroma of that liquor takes me back to those moments.

Eventually, the fighting did stop. Mum left Dad for another man and a better life. I was fifteen. My two older sisters had moved out already. Mum thought my younger sister and I would automatically come and live with her, but we both stayed with Dad. I didn't want to leave home and I had no intention of starting a new life with another man I hadn't even met. Home was home, and I only wanted one Dad. For the first time in my life, the weekends arrived and I went to bed knowing that I would go to sleep and not wake up to those violent episodes. It was the strangest feeling. But that peace left an empty void in our lives. A broken home is the loneliest place on earth. The smell of fresh baked cake after school drifted off into the past. Dinner time slowly became TV dinner time. Life changed for the better and for the worse. Mum was gone. Life seemed so cruel. We'd get carted across town for nights at Mum's new place with her new partner, but I held him responsible for breaking up our family. I always thought: *How could any man turn up and take a woman away from her family? How could he sit there and talk to me as if that was the way it's always been — him and us?* I couldn't look him in the eye — ever.

My traumatic childhood episodes seemed to pass like a series of bad dreams. Our snug suburban life deteriorated and Dad seemed to have given up on life. Discipline went, advice went, and adolescent bonding with my role model never came. He went from caretaking an entire office block in the city to caretaking a water pump at the local hospital, working twenty-four hour shifts, where he just sat alone in the pump house, solving jigsaw puzzles and drinking Scotch whisky. And, at home, he drank more Scotch whisky. Johnny Walker is a name embedded in my mind. Dad would sometimes call Mum when he was drunk to tell her he loved her. It was the only time I heard those words between Mum and Dad. But it was too little too late. Mum was gone.

Our living standard dropped and we were forced to seek government housing assistance. We were offered a small unit in a complex close to Maroubra beach. It was your typical Housing Commission enclave — grassless lawns, fly screens half hanging from windows, a public phone that was always vandalised, and loud and rough neighbours. We were surrounded by a treasure trove of victims of society — single mums, with up to four kids from as many fathers, who took advantage of generous government allowances for having to endure such harshness, heroin addicts, dealers, drunks, divorcees, immigrants, and the unemployed or the unemployable.

We were the bane of society thrown together so society would always know where the collective losers were — and we also would know who we were. Here I was, a well-mannered, young private school boy from a very discerning suburb suddenly thrown in with a new, and very different, crowd. Adjusting to a new way of life, I gravitated to the kids in my neighbourhood as young people do. Running undisciplined and unrestrained, the beach, and eventually the local pub, became our home. We became our own family and set the rules accordingly.

Leaving school, jobs were here and there. I had big aspirations at school, but I became a product of my environment and, after moving to the housing estate, I never really strived to achieve anything grand. I never had any resistance to work, as I always seemed to find it, but I could never apply myself to the nine-to-five routine, as I found this suffocated some desire for freedom churning inside. If I found that my freedoms were compromised, I'd leave. Mowing lawns at the local golf club, carting slabs of tobacco at the local cigarette factory, storeman, loading planes at the airport — none of them took me anywhere but back to the unemployment office and then back to the beach. The beach was the magnet for us all and the weekends a cherished moment to let loose with everyone. It was the elements — the beach, the ocean and the sun — which nurtured me, kept me fit and looking healthy, but masking what I had begun to get up to.

2. Gotcha!

AH, THAT FIRST INHALATION of marijuana with its aromatic fragrance and the toy-like bubbles as they churn in the bong. Bravado was paramount in the company of my peers. Trying to look every bit the seasoned pro, that explosive cough as the smoke filled my supple lungs could not be fought back and, with every cloudy gasp, ruptures of laughter overcame my mates as they urged me on. Time and practice would condition me to my new social thrill, as I worked in earnest to condition my lungs and keep pace with the others, enjoying the giggles, the munchies and the cool persona I was feeling. That addictive hit of drawing back each burst of smoke on the bong, feeling the charge of the mini-fireworks display of cinders descend down the hose to be extinguished in the rancid water, was what we all seemed to yearn for — that moment of ignition and the smoke to billow. We bestowed the highest honour upon this coolest of plants, treating it like gold, as it began to hold us together, and indiscriminately and passively hold us to it.

Drugs like pot were everywhere, which made them seem normal — part of how the adult world worked, or at least a part of how our world worked. They were so cool. Aged sixteen, I saw getting stoned as no different from Dad and his mates sneaking a cigarette and a beer behind their fathers' backs. Everyone was doing it. Plus, Dad now being an alcoholic, and my role model, sent the right messages. It was 'user, try at your own risk' and it didn't matter if you were from government housing or chauffeured around every day. My generation's covert vice of pot was a classless domain, which had woven its magic into our corner of suburbia.

As my head grew accustomed to this daily haze, a new perception of life was emerging. At times, I had to repress weird feelings of paranoia, as it was by no means hip to lose one's cool and freak out. It was just like drinking too much. Too much alcohol and I'd throw up; too much pot and I'd get paranoid. Anyway, the fragility was rare and to opt out of a session due to weakness was never an option. My world — working, surfing and spending time with the family — had to accept my numbed-out coolness, as I became stoned during the week and hung-over from alcohol on the weekend. Excitement was drawn from my raw youthfulness, bursting with energy and a new pack of mates rough and ready, all hell-bent on pushing our coming-of-age towards anything that would get our adrenaline pumping and our testosterone firing, consuming whatever was the way of the day.

The guys down the beach were taking it *all* on — big waves, beers, brawls and bongs, with the latter a passive counterbalance preventing many ending in jail or a wooden box. For now! I went along with the collective way, not thinking of anything other than being one of the boys. Our new weekly hangovers were trophies of a big night out — the sorer the head, the better the night. Come Sunday, friends would gather to exchange bravado stories of who shagged who, who fought who and who felt the worst. Our sullen faces were pasty and gaunt, with a disturbing green tinge. But after a few hours' surfing, we once again looked like paragons of youth and health.

Scoring for others and 'taxing' a nice bud from the deal, midnight raids on growers' backyards, and tearing sanctified crops from their secret shelters, were cheap and thrilling ways to keep our bowls full. Soon it was dodgy deals with all sorts of misfits from all corners of town. In the pursuit of our beloved leafy gold, trouble was never far, and we were ready for it.

'Wait here, I can't let you see where my mate lives,' ordered some guy who turned up to the beach one day. We had driven in his car to the other side of the city to score. I handed over my money and he told me to wait for him at a nearby bus stop. He then drove off. Two hours passed and the realisation of a deal gone bad had my fury explode. I ran like a marathon man for miles till the anger subsided. Mob rule was always the policy in the lawless domain we began to revolve around. In this game, trust was earned and deceit was neither forgiven nor forgotten.

On occasion an opportunity would allow me to personally rebalance the scales of karma, though not in a saintly manner, but satisfying nonetheless. As I walked into my local pizza restaurant after a drinking session at the pub, I was puzzled by the hefty man sitting to the side of the counter. The restaurant, with its cheap plastic chairs, cheaper plastic, chequered tablecloths and plastic roses was half full of patrons eating pizza, which only really tasted palatable when drunk because they were either soggy or overcooked and as hard as frisbees.

I knew his crumpled face, devoid of feeling, but I couldn't think of where. Then it came flooding back. My heart began to pump feverishly and my instinctive fight or flight impulse made its decision. I casually walked up to the thug-like crook, twice my size, twice my age and twice as ugly. Relaxing ever so casually in his chair, with a smart-ass look on his face, I noticed his hands were draped with ponderous rings that in the street-wise world said, 'I'm ready!' But there was no time now for rational thinking. I was there in his space. I'd been close to the action of a few fights in the pub, but I was still that well-mannered private school kid and, to date, hadn't found the courage to start swinging punches. Enduring violence for so long in the family made me withdraw and get nervous from even a heated argument. I used to change the TV channel when people started arguing in a movie. But there I was, now faced with a true moment of manhood: man versus man. To retreat now and cower away would have made me a wimp, and allowed this guy to hang out on my turf, forever belittling me.

'Do you remember me?' I asked, trying to subdue the fear rippling through my words.

'What!' his size and age enough to convince him of his

superiority, as he eyed me with a look of invincibility. It was a look I projected back, as my eyes widened, the fury inside hardening my stare.

'I'm the sucker you left standing at the bus stop.'

Before he had the chance to absorb my final word, I landed a crushing blow plumb on his cheekbone, splitting open his acne-scarred face. Blood sprayed instantly all over both of us and I continued with a barrage of lefts and rights, some connecting beautifully as if the debt was being reduced with each infliction of pain. I could hear patrons screaming, but my focus was unmoving — he was mine. There was no fear now, no thoughts and no mercy. I couldn't believe that he didn't fight back. He succumbed to the onslaught, curled up on the floor screaming like a child. I began to ridicule his cowardice. With a couple of parting kicks to the body, which were more demoralising for him than vicious from me, I casually walked back to the counter, apologised to Tony the owner, who had seen many a skirmish at his restaurant, ordered a pizza and returned to the pub.

My five-minute conquest was that of a hero and my blood-stained shirt the nectar of the battlefield. I had entered manhood and my standing among my peers was instantly elevated. Surfing, women and fighting were the benchmarks for status. My girlfriend had tarnished my evolving ego by sleeping with a number of guys behind my back, but fighting restored it. I really was now one of the boys who commanded respect.

About a month later I entered the same pizza restaurant and to my amazement the guy I left there wailing on the floor was seated with three companions. By the time I noticed them, they were all pointing towards me, their number an obvious advantage. I panicked and thought that this saga is far from over. But it was my hometown and I quickly realised that there were three choices: stay and get beaten up; run if it looks like I'm going to get beaten up; or finish it here. I came to the conclusion that *if you want to play with a three-to-one disadvantage, wait one moment.* Very casually, I strolled back out and re-entered the smoke-filled pub across the road, full of any number of takers for a good fight, and requested some help. The boys were ready, like racehorses about to explode from the barrier. By the time the group exited the restaurant, about eight of us were waiting outside, the adrenaline swirling among us. Our opponents had looks only their mothers could love. They were covered in tattoos and they were bigger than us, but their size advantage didn't intimidate us. Like surfing big waves, we were ready for the rush, but nervous at the force moving towards us.

No words were spoken; it abruptly erupted into street violence. Both sides wanted on! Overwhelmed with the athleticism of hard-core surfers, our opponents scattered and the guy who ripped me off raced down the street and I took chase. He ran like prey on the prairie and, as I was closing in for the kill, he turned suddenly and entered an open front door of *someone's* house. We both ran down the hallway and through the lounge room where a couple was seated watching television.

'Call the police. Call the police,' wailed my combatant, his voice fraught with fear.

'What the fuck are you both doing?' beckoned the male house owner, while his partner screamed at his side.

We raced by them and, to my adversary's misfortune, he entered the bedroom. There was no escape. I flew through the air, tackling him onto the bed. Another pitiful submission followed. Again, he screamed and curled up on the bed. I stood victorious over the top of him and a rush of satisfaction elevated me. I had taken his power, crushed his strength and destroyed his ego. I suddenly realised I was in a stranger's house, standing on their bed over some guy curled up sobbing and dripping blood over it. Embarrassed, I walked out past my accidental hosts, apologised for the inconvenience and went back outside, by which time our rivals had run off into the night and the fight was over.

Like dogs who have fought and reclaimed our piece of turf,

we all went back to the pub and drank to our success. We were metro-tribal warriors, feasting on the story and collective experience of our social slaying. The camaraderie we solidified was that of a brotherhood, to be continually reinforced through our like-minded antics. Proud of who we were and where we came from, our suburb signified a way of life. Maroubra was a tough part of town and I was now well and truly a local lad. With such a fired-up attitude, it was only a matter of time before the long reach of the law grabbed hold of us. Deciding to move out from home with three close friends — Brian, John and Mark — we rented a cheap unit opposite the beach. Now we had our own pad, which ended up being everyone's. Every afternoon after work, bodies would stream into our place and it would turn out to be one serious session. We were well catered for. Friends who were selling pot plied their trade at our place. Their fee was to keep our bowls always full.

It wasn't long before we were evicted, and so we moved to another cheap, cockroach-infested flat, about a kilometre away. Our previous unit was fully furnished. The new one wasn't, and so we decided to go and take what was needed. Donning black, we made a 3 a.m. raid on the old unit, using a spare key not returned. Brian, who had a body chiselled from stone — and the way he used to always fight when he was at the pub, I was sure he had rocks in his head — needed a mattress. We placed the double mattress onto the front lawn and stacked it with whatever wasn't nailed down. Grabbing a corner each, we hauled the mattress through the streets, piled high like a pyramid, at times falling over in stitches of laughter as bits and pieces fell off, echoing into the silence of the night. Next morning we redecorated our new place with curtains, rugs and cutlery — with everything but the kitchen sink, although we did take the plug.

A couple of days later, John, being twenty-one and the oldest of us all, came rushing into our bedrooms at about six in the morning urgently whispering, 'The cops are coming into the unit.' We grabbed all the contraband lying around. Bongs, cones and pot quickly got thrown out the side window. John had started growing a crop in the hallway, taking advantage of the sunlight there. The plants, about a dozen in all, were about a foot tall and looking well loved. John tore the plants from their pots and raced to flush them down the toilet.

Because I was the one who was the persuasive talker, I was urged to answer the firm knock at the front door. One of the officers said that they were investigating the theft of household items from a unit nearby. With a look of curious innocence, I told the officer that it's fine, that we have locks on all the doors and windows, but thanks for letting us know. As I was talking, another officer took a peek inside and saw all the empty pots lined up. That was enough for them. Before I knew it, four of them were inside the unit. We were told to stay put while they looked around. One of the officers walked into the bathroom where John was rinsing his hands after sending the contraband down the toilet: 'Do you mind, mate?'

The officer apologised and closed the door and told him to hurry up. John came out and said, 'Thanks. What's the problem?'

On closer inspection of the empty pot holders, one of the officers picked up one of the pots where bits of withered marijuana leaves were stuck to the soil. 'Cultivation of a prohibited item! We have evidence!' he said, waving the pot holder in our faces.

We were all standing in the hallway while the officers searched the unit. For a moment we were unsupervised. John made a swoop for the evidence. He scooped up the leaves and ate them. When one of the officers returned, he saw that the evidence was gone and screamed at us, 'Where's the evidence?'

John said, 'What evidence?' smiling with bits of marijuana stuck to his teeth like remnants of parsley after dinner.

The enraged officer took hold of John's shirt and screamed,

'You little bastard, you ate the evidence!'

John grabbed him back and next moment they were both on the ground wrestling. The other officers came to assist, as John was getting the upper hand, and I was starting to really panic. Finally, it took the four of them to subdue John the old-fashioned way, slamming him repeatedly into the floor and a few kicks to the body. He was handcuffed and then a complete search of the unit was undertaken. The police found the items we threw out the window and then allocated something to each of us for the judge — a couple of bongs and cones. Mark worked at the Department of Defence storage depot as a storeman and he had stolen an Australian flag the size of two king-sized beds. One of the officers became quite intrigued by it hanging from the wall and said that it would look good in his son's bedroom. We were ordered to take it down and carry it to the police car.

Ironically, we were not charged with taking the furniture, but we were ordered to carry it all back within twenty-four hours. No doubt the police, or the owner of the unit, could see we were young and stupid and in need of a good kick in the rear. Again, we loaded up the mattress and hauled it back through the streets. A week later we were evicted once more and we decided that our stint at independence needed to be put on hold. We all moved back to the ease of home. My first criminal conviction: possession of an implement used in the smoking of a dangerous drug. In other words, I got lumbered with the cone. I had just turned eighteen.

The stage had been set and the pace too. It was full throttle into adulthood and my friends and I — my entire beach community — lived, not in the moment, but for the moment — any moment that would bring us together to push ourselves to the limit. Surfing, fighting, drinking, drugs — any release would satisfy that thirst for excitement and an escape from boring normality.

3. Rock rules

MUSIC WAS ALWAYS a motivating medium and the latest underground bands from around the country and the world continually found their way into our car stereos. It was the '80s and rock ruled the airways, and the pub band scene was where everyone found a tantalising convergence of raw adrenaline and musical harmony. I learnt acoustic guitar with some mates. It was a mellow way to chill out when stoned, but it wasn't long before we were jamming a tad more intensely with old, beaten-up electric Fenders, Marshal amps and Tama drums. With an inherent knack for holding a beat, I swapped the guitar for the drums, and with four friends learnt some covers and began playing at the local pub every month.

We called ourselves 'Action Incorporated'. For a covers band, we were tight and played hard, although Mark, the front man, couldn't sing happy birthday in tune, let alone Metallica, AC/DC and the like. But he was one of the boys and what he lacked in talent he made up for in showmanship. He was a classic rebel-type of front man and wouldn't lift anything other than his mic and a bourbon, while we all lugged our gear week-in, week-out. Ted, his brother, was the rhythm guitarist. Ted was a mad Kiss fan and he and I found a great connection musically. Ray was the lead guitarist and an absolute freak. He could copy the exact leads of any of the greatest lead guitarists in the world, note for note, which would leave us all dumbfounded. And Lee, well, he was the bass player and a bit of a loose cannon. He was one of the easiest guys to get into an argument with, and he was as exciting on and off the stage as a church service. But he knew his stuff and we all used to enjoy taking the piss out of him because he was so easy to rile up. Our monthly gigs continually overstretched the pub's security as hundreds of people from all corners of Maroubra piled in and let loose. Many times, the unsuspecting from afar would come and try to muscle in, only to be set upon by a horde of crazy locals, never to return.

In need of a dedicated space to practice, we approached the headmaster from the local high school to ask if we could use the auditorium. He gave us his blessing and the key. Every Saturday afternoon we would thrash out our tunes. It wasn't long before the beach got a whiff of where we were and, before long, Saturday in the school auditorium was the place to be. One day, we got a rude shock when the headmaster turned up. There were people everywhere — drinking beers and bourbon, and skateboarding across the hall. The smell of pot filled the air. About ten guys were bouncing on a trampoline like clowns, kung-fu kicking each other off. The headmaster, teetering on heart failure, got the parting kick by kicking us all out. Obviously, we left the key behind and didn't ask to return. We were that type of band; trouble always followed us.

The Battle of the Surf Bands was held in conjunction with a major surfing tournament in Sydney and we entered the contest. First prize was $1,000 — not exactly *Australian Idol*, but we wanted to play anywhere anyone would let us. Each band, six in all, was allowed one song only. Held at a suburban RSL club, the auditorium was packed with major surf dignitaries, industry representatives and guest celebrity judges — and, of course, our ever-present three hundred-plus entourage from the beach, with the guys all dressed in their fish-net slip-on shoes, faded denim pants, brown belts and striped shirts.

We took to the stage with a hero's welcome, our beach by far the most represented and the rowdiest. After blasting out our Metallica cover, the adrenaline took hold of us and, with that mad look in our eyes, Ted yelled out a song and I clicked my sticks and we launched into another song. The crowd loved it. The organiser raced onto the stage and was yelling for us to stop and get off, but we rolled our heads to the beat and finished with the sound mixer shutting us down. No matter what or where, we always had to break the rules.

We left the stage to the crowd chanting, 'Action. Action.' When we entered the band room, the organiser was quite perturbed, to say the least.

'You little pricks are disqualified,' he said, almost frothing at the lips.

Mark, in the tradition of great front men, replied, 'We didn't come here to win; we came to be remembered.' The words of 'Action. Action' were still piercing the air as the next band was preparing to play.

The big moment arrived and the organiser couldn't wait to get up on stage to tell the crowd we were disqualified. Well, telling that to three hundred of *our* supporters was a brave act. It was duck for cover as beer cans and anything that would make a useful projectile was hurled towards the stage. Pandemonium broke out to the sound of 'Action. Action.' The presentation was cancelled as all dignitaries fled the scene. Afterwards, we were told that we would never again play at any surf function in the country and, understandably, that club.

Jobs continued to come and go, but the band was the only constant in my life for about five years. A few of the guys down the beach started to get into heavier drugs such as speed, cocaine, acid and heroin, and pockets of smaller groups began to do their own thing with the drugs they were getting into. The guys into acid did their own thing, the coke crew did theirs and the few we knew who were taking heroin — although denying it — well their drooling speech and dodgy personas told a lot. There were also a few guys who tried some type of Mexican plant and their minds floated off to another planet and didn't ever look like they were coming back — and they never did. But the beach held everyone together, regardless of what the vice was, and our band brought everyone together.

For me, it was still pot and alcohol. I didn't feel any desire or pull towards anything harder. Pot was still grown outdoors and nowhere near as potent as the hydroponic buds that eventually became the standard. I had a mate who sold pot a couple of suburbs away and in the Housing Commission estate everyone became aware that I could score good 'mull'. I was constantly travelling back and forth to my mate's place for everyone, and of course deducting my fee of a nice bud. That kept me from having to buy pot for myself. Soon my mate just gave me ten deals to save me the hassle of coming so many times. Before I knew it, I was selling to the Housing Commission community. It was more free pot than free money, and for the first time I was running my own small business — albeit illegal. Keeping a float for the next ounce was always a challenge, as everyone always wanted credit and had lame excuses for not being able to pay, and I was never the knock-down-your-door type — not to my friends, anyway. I remember one day arriving home from work, and shortly after hearing a knock at the door. Dad was always too drunk to care about anything other than his next drink, but he wasn't stupid, yelling out, 'Paul. Shop time.' He didn't care.

Life continued on in a wild and carefree way and the band played on, but music seemed to become the same-old same-old — playing to a mad group of supporters who would end up trashing everything and everyone in sight, and getting barred from more and more venues. It all began to get a bit too much. Word had spread across the Sydney pub scene that we were trouble after our band got into an altercation with a major Australian band that we supported one night. The melee was more push and shove, which happened back stage after they finished playing but, as always, trouble was ever present.

The tight outfit we once were on and off the stage began to strain. Mark became so full of bourbon during a performance that his voice became embarrassing and Lee turned into a speed freak, on-edge and ready to tear anyone's head off. Being the drummer, I had to keep my head together, at least until we finished playing, and their antics began to really piss me off. It all culminated where it began, at our local Maroubra Bay pub. Lee began arguing with me because I didn't want to do a fourth encore. He was that pumped full of speed he just wanted to keep on going. I eventually told him to fuck off and he unclipped his bass strap, placed it on its stand and walked up to the drum kit urging me to take a swing. I told him to leave it, but he wouldn't. So I stood up from my stool and landed one right on his nose. Of course, the crowd — all of our friends — loved it. The rest of the band stood motionless. Obviously, we were finished for the evening. I pushed Lee out of the way and went to the bar and ordered a Southern Comfort and soda. We were all good friends and Lee later apologised, but that was enough. Five years banging out covers became a bit stale and we were never going to reach the heady heights of iconic rock. I needed to look for greener pastures.

One long weekend in Sydney, when I was about twenty-seven, friends were going to a dance party in the city and insisted I come and experience something so amazing that it had to be seen to be believed. It was Sex, Drugs and Techno.

4. Dance party

IT WAS A LONG WEEKEND and the Hordern Pavilion, just a short walk to the city's club strip, was playing host to today's youth, today's new way. Black, white, gay, straight — nobody seemed to care one iota. All that was needed was the right attitude — a collective anticipation of an evening that was beginning its ascent to somewhere uniquely special. My first experience of taking ecstasy was one of those moments that I'll cherish for life. Like losing my virginity, I will always know where the passage took place, with whom it was shared and the virtuous, amiable feelings. As we approached the Hordern Pavilion, I felt trepidation, nervously looking for any internal sign that I was succumbing to the alluring spell of 'E'. 'Can you feel it?' was the mantra from friends, as I probed all corners of my body awaiting those much-talked-about sensual triggers.

The smell of the latest colognes wafted through the highly energised air. The uber-chic glamorous were scantily clad in designer names and unique op-shop creations that would rival any major label. It was a new scene and looking like a totally new way of life. Clamouring towards the turnstiles with this alternative and cool-looking crowd, I was beset by a heady feeling of excitement. People's eyes were wide and pinned, and a surreal beat in the distance began to roll everyone's hips.

Walking into the complex, the cool evening breeze was flowing freely over my torso when this strange tingling sensation filled my body. From my irretraceable core, some pulsating sensual wave kept splashing to the surface, emanating out to the world around me. With the wind riding over me it was like every atom was a tiny feather lightly caressing my skin. Everything began to look so clear, so crisp and so beautiful. My eyes felt like they had never felt before, with euphoria and a deep presence emanating from my omnipotent gaze.

As the physical reactions kept building, I began to feel this immense surge of love firing from my heart. It was becoming a truly alchemic experience as my heart, my inner love, poured out to the world around me. My friends were also entering that unique lucid zone and we unashamedly began telling each other how we all treasured the mateship we had. The genuine brotherly love I was feeling for them was overwhelming, having never exchanged anything other than a slap on the back previously. This amazing night's journey was only beginning, as we followed the pilgrimage closer to the action. It was without a doubt the most amazing experience of my life and I couldn't believe I had not embarked upon such an incredible odyssey till now. I was alive, as every part of me shone and tingled, like the world's entire beauty was channelling through me and back out through my heart. The ecstasy was unlocking some inner illuminate, overriding all of my anger, stress and fears, and I was touching on something very deep and immensely powerful. I wondered, with the innocence of a child's joy: *How can something so small and insignificant give me such an out-of-this-world feeling?* For the first time in my life, I was feeling what it truly meant to be a loving human being, connected to everyone and everything around me, and I consciously acknowledged the dawning of a new chapter in my life. Bar room brawls and rock music were no more.

As we neared the main arena, I was besieged by a confidence not experienced ever before. In the distance I could hear, and feel, the pounding of this new style of electronic music, which magnetically drew me in. Entering into the darkened surrounds, the music, the lights and the crowd made it seem like I was in some sci-fi movie set. The ensemble and the ecstasy had me thinking that the entire experience had been painstakingly put together piece by piece just for me. It was my night.

As I commandingly gazed spellbound from the terrace down onto the dance floor, the opaque sea of bodies was synergising into a type of mystical field as the haze and laser lights glistened above everyone's heads. My eyes momentarily began to get heavy and sleepy. Shutting them isolated the music. *The music, my God, the music. So crisp, and so clear!* That thumping boom-boom vibrated through me. My legs became heavy and wobbly. I felt myself entering into a wave of blissful euphoria, slipping in and out of clarity and sleepiness, and then suddenly wanting to dance and feel my body move, as the mellifluous night continued its exultation.

The enduring clarion of the music maintained the chamber, with the collective plateau in a trance-like state. It was tribalism — millennium style. The core of this kaleidoscope of people was predominantly gay, thronged tight in a sweaty, shirtless amour. The fringes of this mass of bodies were more or less hetero, wearing less provocative clothing. A continuum of movement ebbed and flowed from the unified pack, casting a misty mosaic across the hall. There were glamorous women everywhere, stylish guys and everyone danced so cool, erotically swaying from the hips as bodies comfortably, blissfully and often seduc-tively slid off each other. With the pills peaking collectively, the energy — some unique energy that this dance party crowd exuded — fused us all as a single loving movement. With hearts pouring open, desires became contagious and some type of invisible magnetism linked many to subliminal matches through the crowd. Gay found gay, straight found straight, and bi's found whoever they could. Perfect strangers seemed to float into each other's embrace. Life felt so perfect. All of my weekday baggage was a world away from that moment. *This is what it is all about. The world is a beautiful place, especially here, now.*

Feeling one with all, I believed that I *did* deserve the most beautiful woman there. My desire came, not from the old hardened male ego determined to conquer, but through some overwhelming desire for love and intimacy. I brazenly walked up to the most amazing woman I felt I had ever seen. An encapsulating spark from her eyes stunned me. Without a tremble or an intimidating urge, I placed my hands on her hips and whispered into her ear, 'I love the way you move.' She slowly turned and looked into my eyes, mirroring the same deep presence, and whispered into my ear, lightly stroking it with her soft lips, 'Show me the way you move.'

I had no inhibitions, no fear and no underlying intentions. She was looking at the real me — clear, confident and open to a genuine human interconnection. Hypnotised by each other's gaze, we suddenly fell spontaneously into an intimate, passionate kiss. Immersed in the energy of the crowd, but cocooned in our own ardent impromptu, we savoured our moment — dancing, embracing and talking. I realised that life was certainly more than I believed it to be.

To cruise around the fringes of that hazy array was like a ride on some fairytale merry-go-round, taking in all of the physical and energetic beauty on show, innocently stumbling into strangers. But it didn't matter; there was no aggro atmosphere in a place like that. *Not at a dance party.* Everyone was floating, bound within their own harmonic climax, and anchored to the most poignant of communions. An amble to the bar for some much-needed water was a task that required urgent delegation. 'Can you tell me, is that a five or a fifty?' But no one cared about my temporary ineptness. Worries now were well and truly a world away.

The toilets were a kind of time-out bonding area. They lacked any of the decorum or glamour people were so eager to exude upon arrival. Gender was one and the long queue offered an opportunity to build upon that special party camaraderie. A snort of coke with the crew, sex with a stranger — it didn't seem to matter. Everyone was living in the moment. I was witnessing the discarding of social protocol; don't judge, don't worry and don't be shy. Total strangers were satisfying their primal sexual urges in the confines of a cubicle, and then simply and easily parting in opposite directions, blissfully reflecting upon that moment of pure ecstasy, savouring the innocuous but beguiling state of sensual freedom that this party's ticket bought.

Around 6 a.m. the steady and slow flow out into the sunrise had everyone reaching for the number two dance party essential — sunglasses. The morning azure brought me down a level or two as my body began its descent, sending strange signals that it had had enough for one night. Fragile and exhausted, it was time to call it a night. I was unable to project any of the charmed power I had felt earlier. My body seemed to be spasmodically quivering in some type of after-tremor, trying in earnest to realign itself to normality. It was time now to slump with the bodies prosaically laid across the ground and take in the crowd from behind the safety of my shades.

For many, the morning was only the halfway mark, as the city played host to numerous long weekend recovery parties, pushing clubbers on into the day with that continual thumping beat still pulsating through their system. For those avid soldiers of the night, fighting the impending onslaught of their stupefied state, a top-up of pills, coke or speed and a nice joint set the scene to bleed every bit of the weekend from the calendar. It was the epitome of freedom and free choice. It was an extreme expression of my generation's social idiom. Too tempting and too seductive to pass by, music and drugs were the driving force to push on into the day, as those seekers of pleasure converged on the inner city, scurrying to the darkness of another venue, fanatically clinging onto that blissful state of being.

For me, my first dance party had ended. The jaded journey home seemed like an eternity, as the night became a distant blur. My body had well and truly had enough for one weekend and my mind was already positioning itself into play, preparing for the uncertain days ahead. *Was it worth it? It was.* **This** *is now what we do.* **This**, *today, is who we are.*

'See you at the next one.'

5. Coming down

THE ILLUMINATED WORLD of ecstasy and its supportive culture was like my first romp through a toy store as a child. New stimulations and inner feelings of joy tantalised my senses to an extent that *that* place was where it was at. That place was special, beyond the blandness of daily life. It was not an abstract experience. It was reality, to be yearned for and fantasised about and somehow connected to as often as possible. It was Monday noon before my eyes opened from some much-needed slumber. A startling reality slapped me in the face. *Whoa, I bled that weekend and now the weekend bleeds me.* Fragile, hazy and flat, I dragged myself slowly into the remains of the day, though I knew the drill. I'd endured countless hangovers in the past and the new-and-enriched comedown should be fine. It was a part of the ride that I had heard about and time seemed like my best and only ally for the days ahead. I was trying to get my scattered head around the course of the weekend. *The party was Saturday night, I arrived home Sunday morning, and now it's Monday afternoon. So much for work. I'd better call to let them know that I won't be in tomorrow.*

As I gathered my senses, I realised that the old hangover had just leapt to a new level. I felt quite depleted, my body and mind were in a very precarious state. I could feel the ecstasy grinding its way through me, clouding my enthusiasm and deterring me from any physical exertion or social contact. It made the laziness of pot pale in significance. I noticed some rancid stench exuding from the palms of my hands. My body felt and smelt tainted and fouled. New sensations of pain appeared in my back and stomach. My eyes felt sensitive and my mind was shitty and agitated. My entire state shuddered as I sought out any stimulus to weather the storm. As the afternoon drew to a close, cravings and desires were like some new force toying with my mind.

Coffee! Food! Sex! Just give me something to get me through... I want them all!

It's cool for now. I'll bounce back. I'm not alone. Everyone was going through the same process. We all shared the same transcendent high, and we would all experience the same low. The high we experienced together; the low we experienced fragile and alone.

Coming down, like a hangover, seemed to simply be an inconvenient passing that couldn't, or wouldn't, stand in the way of my new sense of life. What I experienced at that party was beyond comprehension. It was as though it was a union with God. *How did all of that happen? How was I able to feel the way I did? If that was the real me, then who am I now? But why is it that I now feel like shit? It doesn't matter about now. I must return to that state. I must return to the real me!* I believed that the pills and their mysterious biological reactions released something within me that was lying dormant. There could be no harm, other than coming down, in drawing on those feelings. Those pills were the magic key to a better life; reality was overrated. *Why feel good naturally when I can feel amazing socially?* I pondered.

The lure had found its catch. My friends and I — my generation — were now bestowed a new social elixir. Rock'n'roll was out; electronic was now the way; coming down meant simply getting ready to come back for more. It was more than any pub or band could offer. It was more than a mere pot session or a drunken night. Ecstasy had entered our lives and we began to revolve around the city, the happening clubs, the latest dance music and the team that played the game — looking cool and knowing the way. Like some kind of habitual Saturday night ritual, stumbling out of an inner-city club on Sunday sunrise became as familiar as catching a sunset. It felt like a cathartic journey, coming together with a tribe that was beginning to span the world, all sharing this new level of human spirit — artificially entering into that hazy world of loving, expansive energy.

We were all eagerly seeking to feel the power of the heart that union once again. The chemical surge from those chalky little jewels was my guarantee of a connection to who I was — to who I craved to be!

Not only did I feel it necessary to return to that loving state, but I also wanted all that supported it — the entire scene of clubs, parties, music and a crowd. It was a non-aggressive and glamorous atmosphere where love conquers all. The consequences of coming down were never mentioned or contemplated. Nor would they have been believed. No one had been down our path before, so who could offer advice such as, 'Watch out for this' or 'Take care of that'? Coming down was simply the weekly price of my ticket to freedom from the insular suburban life I was living. It was the liberation of my soul. It was *my* toy shop and I could come and stay for as long as I wanted, as often as I chose.

6. I love you

THE LONGEST JOB I HAD held so far — some three-and-a-half years — was at Sydney Airport working for the now-defunct Ansett Airlines, loading passenger planes. The shiftwork, which allowed me either the mornings or afternoons free, gave me plenty of time to go surfing. Every three or so weeks, I would be allocated a four-day break. Plus, there were cheap airfares. I used to fly to the Gold Coast and stay with a mate living up there, and also to Bali, surfing Uluwatu with all the Maroubra guys and then running amok at the Sari Club.

But the new inner-city scene I was gravitating towards began to take precedence in my life. It wasn't long before my allocated sick days began to run out — mostly used on weekends or Mondays. Loading aircraft, suitcase by suitcase and up to five thousand kilos of freight by hand during a shift, is not the type of work for the weak. I was fit — surfing, going to the gym and swimming — but I could feel that ecstasy was beginning to take the edge off my body's physical strength. One morning I went to work straight from the nightclub, having received two written warnings about poor attendance. I was on my last notice. Partying all night and then hauling tonnes of freight don't mix and, in the middle of a flight turnaround, I felt something pop in my back. I had to be carried to the sick bay.

Tests revealed that I had injured my spine (L5S1) and the facet joints were worn away. The specialist told me quite bluntly that I had better choose another job, as loading aircraft was going to cause permanent damage to my spine. I was off work for a few months and undertook a lot of rehabilitation therapy. I also undertook my own self-medicated pain therapy: partying. Not long after returning to work, my back gave way again and the disc was bulging against my sciatic nerve. Management were convinced that I was simply trying to pull some compo scam, even though the medical tests showed that I was doing serious damage to my back. Some time later I returned to work, and again the pain flared up during the loading of an aircraft and I went home early. That was enough for management. They fired me.

I'd always paid my union fees (they were mandatory), never really knowing what good they did other than to rally everyone for a strike. I was always amazed at how union guys have this ingrained 'us versus them' mentality. I received a call from my union delegate saying that the way the airline had treated me was absurd and he had arranged for me to see a solicitor. After going through my case, the solicitor took off his glasses, placed them on the table and with a winner's grin said, 'I can get you some money out of this.' It was like I was an even money bet.

The solicitor and the union arranged an all-expenses paid court case, which lasted about six months. I was dragged in and out of doctors' and specialists' offices, but, finally, my day in court arrived. This time I was on the winning side. After a scathing rebuttal from the judge and a lot of law jargon, my solicitor, again with that winning smile, said that the other party had offered me a $70,000 settlement: 'Do you accept that?' It wasn't difficult to say yes. I was offered my job back, but it couldn't be loading aircraft. It was a position in the roster department. But that meant Monday to Friday, nine to five. I declined their offer. Finally parting company with the airline, I walked away with an unexpected compensation bonus, plus all my big-business entitlements, worth over $100,000, and thought that it was a good time to go on a holiday. I had never intended to scam the airline, but I was no angel either. On the day I was terminated, I had gone to the staff travel office and purchased an open ticket to Europe for about $100. At the time, I was happy with that for compensation. After the court case, I realised that it was good foresight.

Cashed up, I bid farewell to Dad and his new live-in partner,

Joyce. They were more drinking partners than anything else. My travel plan was alcohol in the Greek islands, ecstasy in Ibiza, and pot in Amsterdam. I began to be intrigued by new-age spirituality because of my experiences on ecstasy. With an esoteric book in hand, I settled into my economy seat and excitedly anticipated the trip of a lifetime. It was an ominous warning though when the plane I departed Sydney in, after transiting Bangkok, experienced a fire in one of the engines. We had to make an emergency landing back in Bangkok.

After an unscheduled night in an airport hotel, I made it to Greece and headed straight to the island of Ios where I met up with a couple of friends from Maroubra. We drank the local brew every day for nineteen days straight. The local brew smelt like paint stripper and tasted how I imagined paint stripper might taste. Each day in Ios was exactly the same as the previous one. Rise in the afternoon, head to the beach to soak in the warm crystal clear Mediterranean water, which allowed us to wash away our lingering hangovers, eat stuffed tomatoes and lamb souvlaki, shower, and head back into the night, ending with either some backpacker under my arm or another lamb souvlaki. We then headed to Ibiza. Checking into a hotel on the beach, I asked the desk attendant if there were any nightclubs nearby.

She said, 'There is one across the road. But the only problem is that it opens at 5 a.m.' My face lit up. I looked at her with a cheeky smile and said, 'Perfect!'

And so *la fiesta Balearic* began. Ibiza was where I got to witness and experience the pinnacle of the scene I yearned for. Cheap pills, the most amazing women I had ever seen, and clubs that made the Sydney dance scene pale in comparison. I dived in and delighted in the orgasmic jostling of all of my senses. I felt like Alice in Wonderland. We spent a week in Ibiza and the only difference to our schedule in Ios was that we never made it to the beach, even though we were staying right on it. Waking too late in the day — or ending too late in the day — clubbing held precedence over everything else. Going as hard as I was, being hung-over and with the coming-downs intense, the holiday vibe and European culture helped me to push on. This was a once in a lifetime experience and nothing was going to derail it.

I parted company with my mates in Ibiza and headed alone to Amsterdam, where the air of the café district was permeated by the smell of marijuana. I couldn't believe the city's open attitude to the drug. I checked in to a run-down backpacker hotel that looked and sounded nothing like the flashy ad in the free magazine I had picked up. But I could smell pot in the air, so it was good enough for one night at least. I was in a sixteen-room dorm and there were some dodgy-looking guys in that room. I could sense that Amsterdam had a villainous undertone to it. Locking my personal effects in one of the hallway lockers, I headed straight to the first café I stumbled across — and, after the intensity of the previous three weeks, I literally did stumble in. I ordered a piece of hash cake, a beer and then shared a joint of this new strain of marijuana some guys were passing around — hydro.

I was stoned from the couple of puffs on the small joint, but I felt that the hash cake wasn't doing anything so I ordered another one. The dude behind the counter was adamant that it was strong gear and that I should wait a little longer, but my selfish bravado was just as adamant. 'Another piece, please.' Well, an hour later, I was so wasted that I was convinced that the entire city was following me — paranoid like never before. Returning to a room full of fifteen other guys was certainly not an option. I thought that the only safe place was the cinema. I purchased a ticket and buried myself in the seat in the hope that by the time the movie finished I would be in a better frame of mind. On walking out of the cinema, the city was still coming to get me so I about-turned, purchased another ticket to the same movie and sat through it again.

When I returned to the backpacker hotel some time around

midnight, I locked my valuables in my locker and then feebly fell to my bunk, welcoming the end of that day. Next morning, when I opened my locker, I realised that all of my personal effects had been stolen. My wallet, passport, airline ticket, camera and the Walkman were all gone. Here I was now, with no documentation, no money and no clarity of mind. I thought I'd better call home reverse charges to ask Dad to call the bank and block my credit cards. That was a call I shall never forget. Joyce answered the phone crying. She sobbed out the words that Dad died a week ago — he had a cerebral hemorrhage at home and died instantly. I felt her words move from my ear to my heart like a bolt of lightning punching me in the chest. Tears exploded from my bloodshot eyes. *Dad was dead?*

I *had* to speak with my sisters and Mum. I was feeling like a lost child, stranded on the other side of the world. Whenever I travelled, I always believed that no news is good news, and so I never bothered to call anyone. They told me that they had been searching for me with the Greek authorities, believing I was in Greece. They said they had to proceed with the funeral in two days time and I had to get back ASAP. So began a frantic race against the clock — to the Australian consulate for an emergency passport, new credit cards and a replacement airline ticket. Within twenty-four hours I had left Amsterdam, promising myself never to return to that city. On the long flight back, there was no reflection of the pizzazz of my holiday in Europe, but what did strike me was the fire on the aircraft leaving Sydney, and the dynamics of the theft. If I had not been robbed, then I would not have had to call home. And I would have missed my Dad's funeral. I remember reading in a book how nothing is either good or bad; it just is. A bad experience allowed me the opportunity to attend my father's funeral.

I arrived back in Sydney and I must have looked quite a mess, as customs searched everything. I urged them to hurry, the clock was ticking. I made it to the funeral with less than an hour to spare. My strained face couldn't mask the loss of Dad, three weeks of intense partying and a sleepless flight. My sisters had notified my friends and they were all there to support me. At the closing of the procession, it was the only time I could recall, other than as a little boy, saying the words to Dad, 'I love you.' *Why didn't I ever tell you that? I could only ever say it to you when it was too late. Why couldn't I ever tell you I love you as an adult? I've been on this ecstasy trip with all-encompassing love, yet I couldn't tell **you** that I loved you, the most important person in my life.*

I did finally tell Mum that I loved her, never really having much to do with her since the divorce. I always held deep resentment that she abandoned her family but, with Dad's loss, now was now, and Mum was there for us. With Dad's passing, I felt a new connection kindle between us that hadn't been there for many years. I could feel her pain, and that she always wanted to be with us. Dad's passing snapped me back to the realisation that I only had Mum left.

After the family wake, I went back to a mate's place and we drank some more and snorted copious amounts of cocaine. It was about three in the morning before I made it home, thinking that this saga could be put to rest — and I was in desperate need to be put to rest now. While I had been away, Joyce's son had moved into our place, into my sister's bedroom. My younger sister had gone to live with Mum because Joyce was quite nasty towards her. Joyce seemed to have some jealousy towards other women, despising my sisters yet treating me like I was the golden boy. Greg, her son, had moved his partner, seven month's pregnant Lauren, into the house as well. Lauren was the type of woman who had a hand in his pocket, but an eye on me. Greg wasn't much better. He had about four kids to four different women and was always whining about what a low breed women are. He was the type of guy who believed that everyone was an idiot but himself. I remember Dad telling me a few times to lock up my valuables because he thought Greg was stealing money from him when he used to stay over.

When I got home, Greg was snoring on the lounge, drunk, with the television on, and Joyce was in bed. Lauren was in my sister's room. It felt like they had really taken over our home. I fell onto my bed, and then Lauren entered my room. She asked if she might sit on the bed and I said sure. She was consoling me and asked to hug me. I laboriously sat up and hugged her. I fell back onto the bed and she began telling me what a wonderful person I was and asked if she could hug me again. I was that out of it and really wanted to — needed to — sleep, but I sat myself up and hugged her again. This time she began kissing my neck and stroking my back seductively with her hands. I was wondering, *Is this what I think it is?*

I pulled away and fell back onto the pillow, and with her hands she opened my trousers and began to go down on me. I was lying there, thinking to myself, *I've just come from my father's wake, your partner is out there snoring on the lounge, his mother is in the room next to this one, you're seven months pregnant with Greg's child, and you're in my bedroom going down on me.* I knew I was an opportunist, but this didn't push the right buttons for me. I told her to stop. She realised that I wasn't keen to explore this forbidden zone and began to apologise. I simply said to go to bed and let me sleep. Next morning she carried on like nothing had ever happened.

I got a bit of wake-up call from Dad's death. It was time to get out of that little Housing Commission flat, which had now been taken over by Dad's partner, her son, and his wanton woman. I realised that, at twenty-nine, I didn't want to hit thirty living in a government unit with an old woman I wasn't related to, a guy I didn't trust, and his partner, with an eye — and a couple of lips — on me. So I moved out and moved in with a couple of friends.

All of our belongings were in that unit — furniture and bits and pieces we had grown up with, as well as Dad's navy memorabilia. Mum took virtually nothing when she left. All our memories were there. Immediately after the funeral, Joyce and my sisters had a huge argument because Joyce wouldn't let them come to take anything. There was nothing of value, just memories. Joyce acted quickly, successfully claiming a war widow's pension as Dad's de facto lover. So a new family fight erupted — Joyce versus my sisters — but Joyce now had the law on her side as Dad's legal spouse. Everything in the house became hers. And still is. My sisters never set foot in Dad's home again after he died. I never really got involved. Things were stirring between Joyce and my sisters for some time before Dad's death, because of Joyce's attitude towards them. I was always treated well by Joyce, but it was more a case of me becoming hypnotised by the inner-city scene. That's where my focus was and that's all I really cared about.

7. Hey Mr DJ

'INQUISITION' DIDN'T GET ANY coverage in the glossy entertainment mags, but for an underground party it certainly pulled a crowd. Once a year, it was the night of nights for the city's ultra-alter gays. On the surface it looked like a crowd of social misfits and deviants, but among the crowd were some of the country's leading artists, designers, and public and government figures. It was a social treasure trove of unique expressions, though all sharing a collective, dark sexual pulse. It was low key, with no photographic equipment allowed inside to protect the identity of public figures and a strict ticketing policy to stop the thousands of mainstream clubbers eager to get into one of the city's best parties.

This was my first major DJ gig, about two years after gravitating further into the Sex, Drugs and Techno scene. I had a DJ friend who had a set of Technics 1210s at home, where I used to dabble competently. I found that mixing came quite naturally to me; being a drummer, holding a beat was second nature. My love of performing with music had returned. But this time it was different. There was no band. It was just me. Dance music took me to another level — to some mystical resonance. It was the electronic, hypnotic rhythms that filled some part of me, oscillating a type of subsonic lure totally complementary to the ecstasy and the entire scene that drew me in. I had honed my musical talent at one of the city's leading hotspots where I played for free before and after the main DJs. I then landed a residency, and my skills and music style were quickly recognised and rewarded with a potentially breakthrough gig — Inquisition at the Hordern Pavilion. I'd partied at the leading clubs in Ibiza and gotten to know the inner-city scene of Sydney, so I thought that this gig would be much the same. With my ego feeling it was getting what it needed, I arrived at the party, carrying my record cases like they were a couple of large trophies for all to see. *Yes, I'm the DJ.*

A pungent smell of body odour lingered in the air. To many, this was an aphrodisiac scent and a stamp of just what type of crowd it was. A Chanel No. 5 crowd it wasn't. There were no flashy egos or fake facades, just a let-go mind-set and an evening to either remember or regret. The daylight-depleted crowd was a raw, primal melting pot of leather, tattoos and body piercing. With topless butch-like dykes strutting with an attitude of testosterone overdose, and yeti-like men with bushman beards and hair from front to back cruising arm-in-arm with almost teen-like, fresh, smooth 'boys', it was the epitome of society's sexual expression and social release.

I was one of four DJs for the night and my new kid on the block status among the other DJs had me relegated to the opening set. But that suited me fine — plenty of time to enjoy the party afterwards. Inside the pavilion, huge speaker platforms corralled the punters, with the man of the moment — me — strategically perched in my pulpit-like booth above the masses, preparing to tune myself into that unique free-flowing energy and take them all on a journey to the stars. I was ready to start this party and drive it into the night. I knew that the right musical atmosphere would be the difference between a good night and an extraordinary event. For me it was more than a music-savvy performance. I inherently possessed the musical talent and, together with an innate understanding of perceptively coalescing music *and* drugs, I was the shepherd, ready to guide my flock through a hypnotic ride on a flying carpet.

The scene from the DJ booth was a sea of skin, smoke and an intangible feeling of energy. The laser lights pierced the thick air, drawing the crowd up and out, while the massive beat I held command of kept all down and dirty. I felt myself connecting deeper to the audience as the set progressed. My fingers formed a sensitive tuning fork resting delicately on my vinyl pressing, as

I readied the arrival of the next track, with each beat being another stepping stone into the advancing vortex. My job was to keep the hips grooving and the heads floating. It was a job I savoured, and an experience unfathomable. Some inner knowing of the consummate energetic power at hand and my ability to move the emotions of the masses with *my* performance was to see me revered in that moment by those who stood before me. My music selection resonated with them and was certain confirmation that I was one of them — that I knew them subliminally.

As I stood at my musical console looking out through the crowd, the drug-hungry were beginning to float off into the illuminated night. Continually anticipating the mood of the moment, the masses communicated their energetic state with me and I answered the calling with a compatible fat, rolling bass line and heavenly harmonics. These were hardened clubbers who knew the Sex, Drugs and Techno scene. They began it all! They knew the energy here and they knew how to get the most out of it. Oral sex was happening right before me, the receiver's lustfulness transfixed upon *me* during this unadulterated act as if I represented some type of rhythmical sexual conduit in my phallus-like DJ booth. People were sniffing on bottles of amyl-nitrate. Sexual stares propelled continually towards me — from all around. The energy from their eyes was bestial and perverted.

Previously, DJing at the main club strip in the city, it was predominantly the gay strip and that's where *everything* happened. I went from homo-phobic to homo-let-me-join-the-party almost overnight. I got to witness first hand how gays were always ready with their sexual prowess. The straight boy with a non-interest persona would have them treat you like a king in the hope of getting lucky. And as a good-looking straight boy facilitating their night, I certainly possessed all.

A party such as this was all about a collective mind-body catharsis, as this entire event was designed with the chemical cocktail in mind. The lights, the music and the crowd all communicated an unspoken language — drugs. Drugs not only for the crowd, but also for me. I was well catered for with free alcohol and drugs offered from one of the organisers, hoping to draw me in deeper to that celestial space. As my set was finishing, I was ready to down some complimentary MDMA powder. It was much the same as E. If an E wasn't available, I'd accept the powder. But a pill was always easier to consume than having MDMA powder congeal in your throat. I handed the turntables over to the next DJ and headed to the toilets adjacent to the DJ booth.

The Hordern Pavilion was built in the 1930s with typically grandiose Art Deco features. A wide set of stairs descended about two long flights, appearing to go deep into the earth and then levelling out to a long and very dimly lit corridor, at the end of which were the toilets. As the pounding beat softened in the distance, a surreal tinkering of the percussion repeated a mantra-like calling through the air, reaching out like connective tentacles. Nearing the toilets, the crowd began to thicken and the atmosphere grew increasingly denser with sweaty bodies acting like a comfort zone of like-minds.

With the crowd as thick as it was and the darkness, there was no determining which were the men's or women's toilets, but by now I took it for granted that the inner-city E scene didn't discriminate whether male or female, gay or straight. I wasn't even sure whether some of this crowd were men *or* women! There was only a single low wattage globe casting a veil of ghostly silhouettes. The heat was stifling, and mixed with an overwhelming smell of body odour. There was now a deftly silence, but for muffled moaning coming from somewhere inside.

As I neared the cubicle I could hear the intoxicated moaning coming from behind one of the doors. I thought, *What's driving me to get off by hanging out and getting trashed with a crowd like this?* A cubicle door opened and I tentatively entered as four men exited, pulling on their nostrils. The space was a cesspit, with the toilet blocked and faeces floating to the top of the rim. It stank like someone had died. Actually, it stank like everyone had died! The only place looking anywhere near clean enough to take a line was on top of the toilet paper dispenser, which had been wiped clean again and again throughout the night by drug-hungry fingers ready for the next user. Maintaining an illusion of sanitary decorum, I opened my wallet and pulled out my driver's licence and perched it onto the dispenser. Then, with my credit card, I scooped out a sizable chunk of the drug and placed it onto the driver's licence. After preparing a line and rolling a bank note, I tried to inhale, but due to the hot, humid conditions the MDMA had begun to dampen and could not be snorted. I had to move to plan B. With my sweaty finger, I stuck it to the pink, now paste-like substance and wiped it onto the back of my tongue, as far back as possible. The taste almost made me vomit. All I had at hand was some gum to stimulate some saliva and deaden the rancid taste now congealed in my throat. It was a means to the end and a few moments were needed to compose myself, as the moaning from the cubicle next to me continued on.

The music magnetised me straight onto the dance floor like some kind of new-age spell. A few songs, a few deep breaths, and that euphoric love-conquers-all feeling had my eyes feeling heavy, yet soulfully piercing. The rolling bass line and tantalising harmonics fed through me. Mixed with the chemical cocktail, I felt I was channelling some sort of heavenly arrival that opened to a blissful appreciation of all around me. Reality was now confined to within the walls of the pavilion, awareness now focused powerfully on this surge of love. I couldn't understand how some strange inner feeling of belonging connected me to this kinky, and influential, crowd. It was like all of us here — the entire inner-city scene — had a secret knowledge of a way to enter into the heart, even though I was puzzled how love emanated in such a perverted-looking and sexualised crowd. I felt I was one with this dishevelled mob, like I was part of a rebellious sub-culture, snubbing our drug-filled noses at what society deemed normal, acceptable and moral. It was my generation.

What seemed like hours passed. The rows of seating spread out along the sides of the pavilion overlooking the dance floor were a perfect gift of rest for the weary. Watching the now-sporadic crowd slowly dispersing from the dance floor, the party was beginning to resemble a pack of extras from a B-grade zombie movie. With the music now a much slower pace, with freakish overtures and the air uniquely heavy and stale, the seating area was now the place to be for those too exhausted to dance and still too wasted to leave. Looking around the pavilion, I was fixated by the absolute raw reality. It was like everybody had entered into some *other* type of reality. There was a group of four women on the dance floor engaged in a four-way tongue kiss, with all hands groping at groins and topless breasts. Some guy was dressed in a morbid clown suit, freaking out those around him who were on Special K and/or acid. Another guy was spread out on the floor near the bar convulsing. A couple of volunteer first-aid officers were placing him into the recovery position, but no one was paying any attention to him. The rows of seats around me were full with people getting it off or simply too messed up to do a thing. Everyone was looking gaunt and anaemic. I sat there blissfully dazed, my deep breaths drawing back the remnants of the drugs.

Remembering that I had still had some MDMA, a gluttonous desire filled my mind once again. I wanted more! I pulled the packet from my wallet, opened it and scooped up the remaining finger full, which was now well and truly paste, again enduring the vile taste to down it with my water. I then pushed my aching back into the seat, placed my feet on the chair in front and awaited, once again, the fuzzy rush from my own inner lucid world. Reality outside of this Sex, Drugs and Techno scene was non-existent. I didn't want the night to end....

And it wasn't going to. At 7 a.m. I headed to the inner city with my music and played at an after party, which was in a closed-off laneway between two pubs. The street was packed with clubbers yet to surrender to drugs or to the night. More free vodkas and E flowed. Totally trashed but remarkably in-sync with the music and the crowd, I was riding *some* type of wave that carried me on into the day. It was like I was feeding the crowd energy, and they were feeding me theirs. I played a six-hour set and I relished this warped moment. I was now paid to create those moments. What a job! What a lifestyle! What a rush! As long as I could hold the music, the crowd and myself together, no one cared what I was on. Everyone was as trashed as me. It was to be party after drug-fuelled party as Sex, Drugs and Techno played on and I had the honour of giving them what they wanted — *my* kick-ass music. And they gave me what I wanted — drugs, the scene and some mystical force that I couldn't get enough of.

It was free entry to every club, with free drinks and drugs. The scene was mine to indulge. The world was mine to take. The stimulation of the music, the drugs, the loose crowds — and the ego — had me living the life of the dance party scene as I became one with it all, letting it take me as high as can be. I thought of how lucky I was and how excited I felt to be able to DJ here and party there, or finish playing and jump right into the action, getting trashed with the boss, my friends, the crowd or just on my own — again and again. I was feeling free, alive and experiencing a lifestyle that I thought only the rich and famous could taste. It was there for me. It was there for all of us. It was ours.

8. Real sex and the city

BECOMING TOO COOL FOR SUBURBIA, the inner-city scene was the place to be, more than just for the weekends. I was drawn to the city's excitement and the close proximity of the many bars and clubs there for work, and play. With the money I received and saved from the airline compensation payout, I had enough for a deposit on a stylish new unit in Darlinghurst. It was in one of the most run-down areas, but so fashionable! Walking distance to party central — Oxford Street — the transformation from suburban boy to metro-sexual was complete. I had a cool pad, a cool job, that allowed me the freedom I needed, and the stamina to keep up the pace — I relished the life I was living.

Peddling deals of pot in Maroubra came to an end as I bid farewell to the beach for the city, mostly because I no longer smoked the new hydro buds, they were too strong and made me too lazy. Plus, everyone was always getting credit and never paying me back. It was time to move on. Ecstasy was now my drug of choice and I could get pills for free by simply turning up to work. But pot wasn't finished with me completely. I played middleman for a woman I knew who wanted to buy hydro — a pound at a time — once a month. She asked if I could score for her and I knew a guy who was growing a crop of hydro in a rented house on the other side of Sydney. He had every room full of the most amazing specimens of horticulture I'd ever seen. If pot were ever legalised, he would certainly win some prestigious awards. It was an easy couple-of-hundred dollars a month — a call from her, a call to my friend, collect, deliver — all in the space of a couple of hours.

DJing began to take me out of Sydney, working interstate, often after meeting venue owners while playing, and also landing a residency at Double Six Club in Bali during the holiday seasons. But it didn't matter where I was, Sex, Drugs and Techno spoke a universal language. And I became fluent in it. The power of ecstasy's loving, connectedness continued to fascinate me. I couldn't understand how that incredible transformation continued to take place. All I could do was enjoy what it did. Yet an incredibly potent, seductive feeling seemed to work itself through the scene. In every bar, club or party, I began to feel this insatiable feeling of lust lingering in the air, which would heighten my erogenous senses, like some animal following the trail of a scent. It was like love and sex were becoming one and the same. Chemical attraction stepped up to another fascinating level. What was once typically a man's domain — chasing one-night-stands — had been taken over by an abundance of women, sharing the same urges and declaring their own salacious needs be met. What I wanted — impulsive, gratifying and no requests for phone numbers — they wanted too.

It was 1 a.m. and I was enjoying a vodka Lambrusco, tucked away, lounging on the back sofa of some Oxford Street bar with a woman whose name I didn't even know. For me, the eyes have always been the most powerful trait in a woman. This woman possessed a powerful and seductive gaze. We both said the right words and we looked cool hanging out together. Plus, I always liked meeting women in gay bars. The macho facade of the straight scene saw a lot of stunning women choose to party in the gay community, where they were spared slurred, cheesy pickup lines by guys holding beers. A lot of my work was in the gay community and the gay scene was where the real style was. Many women liked not knowing whether you were gay or straight and I knew that having a gay question mark lingering always stacked the odds in my favour. As she held a mesmerising focus and moved her body closer, just touching, her body language certainly was sending me an open invitation.

'Feel like a line?' I whispered in a confident tone.

'Sure.'

I furtively led her into the women's toilet with a philandering posture of certainty and empowerment. So far she had made all the right moves with a finale only moments away in the cubicle. In eager anticipation, I could almost taste the sweetness of her lips. I had been down this road many times and knew the drill. *She* held the power and I could tell she loved to see the game play out and see just how smooth I really was. The energy between us was thickening as we stood in line to wait for a cubicle. Once inside our tainted den it was like another world, a seedy boudoir of convenient seduction. The lust was almost electric as I lined the cocaine onto the paper dispenser. The wet and paper-tainted floor added to the bawdiness of our encounter. Slowly, I reached into my wallet and pulled out a crisp $50 note, rolling it like some phallic symbol. Any denomination of lesser value was a coolness point lost.

'After you,' I gestured.

'No, no. After you!' she replied, maintaining an air of safety. I drew back the thick, smooth line, loving the momentary prelude as much as the rush.

She then took it in, stood upright and looked at me with those eyes of confidence and certainty, drawing back the coke with an extended inhalation, then sighing out as if to acknowledge that the demons had been appeased. With her eyes rolling back in an orgasmic ripple, she unrolled the note, slowly licked the cocaine residue from the edge and then placed the note in her purse. She obviously loved doing this, just to see if I had the balls to ask for my money back. It was a real test of my attitude — whether I was the Mr Amazing that I had been portraying. Do I stand my ground and ask for it back and possibly lose my momentum, or does my fear of ruining my chances have me innocently forgetting whose note it was? To my credit I played it well. With a wry smile I smoothly said, 'Enjoy,' the cocaine the primary philtre as I lunged for her palpitating lips. The moment exploded into a fiery embrace within the confines of our unorthodox compartment, as I eased her onto the toilet seat like some type of debauched Romeo, unromantically removing her panties, with them falling onto the muddied floor. She pushed me back and regained her composure as if to stamp her own authority and control over the moment, a stern yet seductive look gesturing out.

As I stood over the top of her, staring down like a victorious warrior, she tilted her head sideways, licked her top lip slowly back and forward, and with both hands slowly began to pull at my belt, at first tightening the leather strap to the point where my Prada insignia began to reverse back and crimple onto my skin. Her face was unmoving, as our game of dominance and submission blended beautifully, as smooth as silk. We both had played out this escapade many times before, inherently knowing when and where to give and take, working our sexual polarities into an explosive magnetic charge.

Loosening my belt and opening my pants, she slid her slender hands inside my jocks. She could wait no longer, moving forward and going down on me with a sexual eagerness equal to mine. I stood there, salivating and ultra-horny through the rush of the cocaine. I then eased her back onto the seat again, and dropped my pants to my ankles, with those too swishing among the septic swath. It was the talismanic crescendo; it was the crème de la crème. With legs sliding in and out from under the toilet door our paradoxical union of the sacred sexuality and sexual sedation filled us both with a hyper-erogenous, intoxicating gratification.

Suddenly, a knock on the toilet door had us both abruptly compose ourselves. She simply kicked her panties behind the toilet; I pulled my sopping pants up with bits of soggy toilet paper hanging from the legs, an offbeat karmic message from the powers above as to the level of finesse I really had. She pulled the door ajar as I stood hidden behind. 'Mind if I come on in and take a pee? I really can't hold on any longer,' said the thirty-something woman with short hair slicked back, though not very visually appealing.

'Sure,' my fleeting partner replied. 'As long as you don't mind sharing.'

The woman walked in and I could sense that she felt the seductive energy within the confined space. She looked at both of us and said, 'Would you care if we *all* share?'

Both women began kissing each other — their tongues battling in a moist, penetrative duel. *What better gift could a man receive?* I couldn't believe my luck. A night on the town and an open mind focused on one outcome could lead to anything. I grabbed the opportunity — literally. As the women kissed, I placed the newcomer's hand inside my pants and then began groping them both. They welcomed my rough, primal clutches. I rolled my head back onto the toilet wall and looked astonished to the heavens above. It was only 1:30, a good start to the evening and, ladies, thanks for the memories. I had to continue on into the night — alone.

Even when I wasn't trying to seduce some woman, there was opportunity always lingering. The scene became pure seduction. It engulfed whatever space partygoers gathered. Every eye in the crowd was ever-ready and willing to connect with those who knew how to play the game and work it well. Women knew the conceited rules of engagement. And the ones in relationships, caught up in Sex, Drugs and Techno, had the hungriest eyes of all, like relationships were some inconvenience, prohibiting all that was on offer.

Playing at a private party for a fashion magazine, I was scheduled with another DJ, who had arrived with his girlfriend. He was to play first. He had that DJ attitude I came across now and again. With his blond trophy in hand and his ego well above mine, he thought he was the greatest musician since Frank Sinatra. I thought, *Mate, we are playing to a crowd that hasn't come to see me or you!* During his set, his girlfriend sat next to me and began chatting. She took a soft hold of my wrist and said, 'Nice watch,' as her fingers continued to caress my skin. I looked into her eyes and those said enough. I thought, *Here we go!* Within minutes we rendezvoused away from the crowd and she whispered cunningly, 'As long as the music keeps playing, we'll be fine.' She then lunged herself at me and it was over as quick as it had begun, possibly a record quickie. She kissed me, thanked me and walked off like nothing had happened. I wasn't even sure it did happen; it was that quick. I innocently cruised back to the DJ booth and said to Mr Sinatra, 'Great set.'

Sex, Drugs and Techno eroded everything — morals, respect, dignity. Any opportunity was evaluated to one outcome — gratification of what I was looking for. The scene continued to fill up with people wanting to explore their boundaries. This was nothing new, as loose sex and voyeurism weren't conceived with my generation. But what was new were the many social outlets to cater to such acts — some open to the public, others strictly behind closed doors. Whatever skeletons lay buried in the closet, there were always avenues to rattle some bones. Being a DJ, I got to play to all types of crowds and got to meet all types of people. Nothing ever fazed me. I'd seen a lot, heard a lot and experienced a lot. I was initially magnetised to the scene through the love and connectedness of ecstasy, but what began to unfold was quite the contrary.

I had a lesbian friend who worked at an exclusive club which catered solely to B&D. She often told me that many prominent figures attended and was amazed at just *who* was turning up. There was no sex, just whipping old men. The pay and tips were great she said, and some of the stories of how these old men got off were almost comical. There was a high profile celebrity who regularly attended. He was the Mr Nice Guy of the older A-list crowd, and his fetish was to be dressed in nappies and placed in a baby's playpen and spanked with a belt. She also told me about one of her gay friends who had been having a secret affair with a senior government minister for years. The minister was married with a family and he lavished his gay lover with money, and secret rendezvous trips to government sponsored exotic places. Another friend of mine was so addicted to massage parlours — the ones with a happy ending — that he needed to attend counselling sessions to try and control his ways.

The gay community had their own steam rooms peppered around the inner city, and, from what I'd been told, they were purely open sex dens, with strangers. During a long weekend in Sydney, the line up of gay men desperate to get in would run out from the laneways and down the main street. And my time at the airport — with the convenience of the cheap airfares — saw us young guys going to Bali surfing, while the older single men headed off to Thailand and the Philippines for sex tours. Throw in the club scene, and I could see how sex certainly sells, and, just like drugs, there were plenty of takers and plenty to share it around.

9. Weekend after 'weak-end'

DJING AND SERIOUS PARTYING were now a way of life. If I wasn't working behind the turntables, I was partying. Now in my thirties, I was habitually pumped full of E at some stage over the weekend. It seemed to have been that way for a few years now, but I wasn't counting. Time was irrelevant. Heading out for the night *never* finished until the following day. The euphoria was too tantalising, the music too entrancing and the scene too seductive to even contemplate heading for *any* exit as I — all of us — held onto that misconstrued feeling we so desperately sought. With accolades, bonds and interludes, I was feeling a paradoxical zest for life shine forth. As the light shone bright though, another force was lurking in the shadows waiting patiently for its own moment of glory. My sisters were all settled into family life, and I was certainly the black sheep of the family. My attachment to youth, freedom and the scene felt like growing up was still running its alluring course. I had no idea where it was all taking me.

Finishing DJing, I left my records in the office like always, popped an E and headed out into the waning hours of the night to one of the many bars or clubs on the Oxford Street strip. Most DJs were too cool to dance but, with ecstasy, I had to dance. In a steamy lather of sweat on the dance floor, suddenly the music stopped and I realised that *another* Saturday night had passed. The air was heavy and stale as seemingly lifeless bodies lay strewn across the surrounding sofas, while us sweaty die-hards left stranded on the dance floor and podiums seemed to be caught way off-guard. 'One more song!' was the unified desperate chant. The ensuing lights created a scattered mental process as to how best to escape the clutches of the night's finale as the drugs were in no way ready to allow me to call it a night. A drawn-out blurry focus on my watch showed 8 a.m.

I couldn't let go of an environment where my inhibitions dropped, social competence flared and I felt so amazing. Denying that my illustrious state could somehow push my system into overdrive, didn't register. Coming down during the week was becoming more intense, but Sex, Drugs and Techno had me as I continued to believe myself to be fine and always in control of my night and my life. And seeing others around me sharing the same journey provided a warped paternal-like comfort. We were more than an urban tribe. We were a weekend family, albeit a very dysfunctional and fragile one, all finding a common chord in seeking to connect to *something* unattainable in the daily grind of life.

My fanatical escapism habitually kept my impervious inner party soldiering on, with a gruelling stamina fuelled with high octane narcotics. At dawn, it was a daylight-avoidant rush to the Day Club, with the line up outside stretching down the street resembling some hand out from a methadone clinic. Even the inch-thick makeup and the slicked-back hair couldn't hide the fact that this was an eerie ticket on a rickety ride called fool's gold. Situated in the dodgiest part of town, the nondescript structure relied on no glossy neon-light marketing. Like a brothel, there was no advertising. Those who needed it knew where it was. It was the bastion of the city, the domain of the damned. Ecstasy had now gone mainstream and moved beyond the city's gay hub. Bikies, gangsters and desperados — everyone ended up at the Day Club.

The ego status of being a city DJ ensured I wouldn't be subjected to the demoralising sight of having to line up as the daunting gladiator figures at the entrance whisked me past the crowd and the speed-filled 'door bitch'. Entering through the metal detector and down the stairs, the mixture of smoke and steamy body odour drew my primal instincts to their rawest, as the instant darkness and thick brume required a few minutes for my eyes to readjust to the motley spectrum I was entering. A cool head and tactical instincts were always needed in a place like that as I had to sift through the conundrums that were before me. *I could get laid or abused. I could score or be arrested. Or I could bump into some guy and end up chatting or swallowing my teeth — or worse. Just play it cool and it will be.* This wasn't the tolerant and soft vibe of the gay scene. This environment was leather, yes, but this crowd's idea of whipping some ass was with a knife or a bullet.

One Sunday afternoon the music stopped way too early and there was a stern announcement that the club was now closed: 'Everybody get out!' On leaving I saw my mate, Karl, sitting propped up on the sidewalk with blood all over him. He had been shot four times on leaving the club by some guy refused entry earlier. Karl was six-foot-four and built like a tank and this guy mistook Karl for a bouncer as he was leaving. After being shot, he lunged at his assailant, took the gun from him and beat him with it till the guy managed to stumble away. Karl then sat himself down and waited for help. I was still so wasted that I was more concerned for my own needs than his. My grasp on Saturday night was not meant to end — at any cost. He was taken to hospital. I took myself to another venue.

The Day Club atmosphere was an intense, edgy environment. The majority male crowd was as hard as nails, pumped full of drugs, and in a tug-of-war of maintaining an E peak and coming down — hard. It was a far cry from the type of crowds that first began to hang out in Oxford Street when ecstasy arrived onto the scene. To be refused entry said a lot about the vibe some people were giving off. Every drug-fucked misfit with some figment of style from all over Sydney wanted in. Every Sunday — and I was there *every Sunday* when in town — the club, with its cocktail of drugs, thumping techno/trance, the intermittent smell of amorous vaginas, an air of aggression and gothic surrounds, would push a jam-packed audience non-stop, all day long. And so I fell deeper into the clutches of that fantasy world, immune to the subtle and gradual descent into the maelstrom. A beer at the pub watching the footy and surfing were a world away. At times I would walk outside the Day Club and be overwhelmed by the reality of the day and hurriedly turn around and cowardly scurry back into the darkness that was my comfort zone — into the darkness that was becoming the signature of my life. That was the Day Club. That was now me. The party couldn't stop. I couldn't stop.

Drugs were as available as the drinks behind the bar, with a greater turnover. Friends were consuming fifteen to twenty-plus Es over the weekend, along with joints, speed, cocaine and bourbon. Being a DJ, everyone felt obliged to fill me full of everything — compliments, alcohol, drugs. I was just some local muso treated like a king in my own sad, little world. It was talismanic, tantalising the esoteric forces of good and evil within me that drew me back again and again, with part of me living in complete denial of the fact that I was living a life that I hadn't even seen on any of the raunchiest TV shows. But my friends were there standing next to me (some just), all part of a larger clan eager to keep the ad hoc script of our generation's new expression advancing into the unknown.

10. Dream on!

THE FACE APPEARED soft and beautiful and then in an instant transformed into a demonic, deformed facade, which engulfed my vision. Slowly, as though it had all the time and patience in the world, a snake slid up from my ankles, curtailing my lower body, sliding graciously over my skin. Its eyes were deep and unpenetrative, transfixed with a cold and airy demeanour. The sensation of its sliding ascension up my inner thigh tantalised my senses, relaxing my mind and preparing me as its victim on its journey from ancient lost souls of the never-never, marching endlessly into the dark abyss of the other side, grooming me as its host with its own alter-love tonic. A dog appeared, standing upright on its hind legs; its head was also disfigured. It grabbed my throat violently and held me down. I tried to move, but I couldn't. Grotesque, midget clowns appeared in the background, laughing and applauding the circus. I felt awake. I was sure I was awake, but I couldn't move at all. *But my eyes are open. I'm looking at the wall. I can't move. What's this holding me down? Am I awake or asleep? I'm sure I'm awake.*

Then suddenly, I rose in a lather of sweat with my heart pounding. The bedroom was eerily silent and a chilling fear filled the air. I lay there numb. My mind would keep me awake for another four hours.

The usual shitty attitude of the waiter didn't seem to register as I sipped on my latte and gratifyingly ate my muffin, my eyes obviously puffy from the lack of sleep the night before — from many nights before. Gazing out into the thoroughfare, the hectic city rush translucently passed by. I sat transfixed upon the horrid dream that somehow touched a deep chord within. A noticeable tremor of my hand as I raised my cup was becoming commonplace. *C'mon! It was just a dream.* It would be the first of many such dreams.

I sat against the window with my back to the other patrons, finding that I was becoming uncomfortable with anyone being too close. I welcomed the almost inaudible sound of the background music, as silence was becoming an uncomfortable state to be, especially in public places. It was like background music was tailor-made for people like me — people who have lost the ability to be comfortable with, and honour, silence.

A bus pulled up to the traffic lights and stopped in front of the cafe window. The advertisement on the side of the bus caught my attention. It was a sexy model, with a *Sports Illustrated* figure. She was dressed in a cheeky devil's outfit with two little horns and a long kris. She was pointing the kris at a male model who was dressed only in a Tarzan loincloth. He was kneeling at her feet holding out a chocolate bar. The caption read, 'Better the devil you know!' I then noticed the bus was full of passengers and it was as though they were all focused upon me. They were judging me and ridiculing the freak sitting in the cafe. My heart began to pound anxiously. *Drive. Drive. Move away.* As the bus pulled away, it left a thick, dark exhaust plume. I numbly stared into the suspended black haze. Peering deeper into the plume, I tried to disregard it, but the thoughts kept coming. *I'm starting to lose my greatest strengths — confidence, centredness and resilience.* I was becoming oversensitive to people and clubs, and the flair of the city was turning on me. Now I could only see chaos in this hectic town. My mind was starting to scare me. I perceived that the CIA was stalking me and my best friend of twenty years was purpose-fully avoiding me because no one answered his phone.

What is going on? People are talking to me and I'm not taking in one word they are saying. And I'm losing my train of thought mid-sentence and forgetting what I am about to say. Things are becoming too intense. I don't have the tolerance anymore to keep pace with this stimulated and altered state. Another one of those things will make me freak out and, whoa, I keep getting these weird hot flushes. My eyes are puffy and teary, my back is completely locked up and my stomach is aching. I seem to be continually so shitty and so fucking depressed that... what's the use? Why bother carrying on for another day? Life is hell. And my mind, I can't stop the morbid and sick thoughts. I'm seeing monsters in people's faces, monsters in my sleep — that's when I do finally get to sleep. My mind is absolutely racing, and it sounds like some type of crazy chatterbox is raving on, and the continual thumping of music keeps playing on and on inside my head, like a drubbing pendulum ricocheting through my mind. Music, erotic desires, burlesque voices, a make-believe dark world — it all just keeps playing on and on. And my best friend, he's fucking avoiding me. He probably thinks I'm a fuckwit. Anyway, I can't stand him anymore. Oh, what's this heaviness I'm feeling? I can't face anyone today — or this week. Fuck, why do I feel like this? Just avoid everyone. Avoid everyone.

And so it goes. Welcome to the fast lane!

11. The Wild West

I WASN'T ALONE IN MY newly acquired negative state. There were others paying the price. Collateral damage was a part of the travails of Sex, Drugs and Techno. Moving to the city had severed my childhood connection to all my mates. I had only a few close friends, who, when I wasn't experiencing bouts of paranoia, I'd only run into at some venue DJing or in the wee hours of the morning. A few vodkas were my tonic for chilling frizzled nerves. But the inner-city scene changed many of us. The beach was our home and there was a time when running wild on our home turf was more innocent, even though we were wild there too. But I had been living the high life of a DJ, with all the trimmings, and I really didn't dwell on the way it used to be too often. There was no need to. I accepted that life was all about me, and the life I had been living only had room for one person — me! Feeling like crap was simply a state I accepted I had to cope with for now and soldier on. Too often though, I would receive a call. The circuit was taking victims. In the '60s it was 'live fast, die young' and to gain that status you were either a rock star or a movie star. What I was witnessing was 'live even faster, die even younger', and 'you' were half the people I grew up with.

We embodied the West. We were the Wild West — hedonistic, distracted, hell bent on consuming, excessive, irresponsible, unhealthy and needing instant gratification. My childhood friend, Mick, dropped out of the main scene, but took drugs into the forbidden zone, ending up addicted to heroin and dying in some railway toilet. Phil got into a fight with a group of bouncers outside a Kings Cross club. They beat him to death and dumped his body in a back alley industrial bin. Troy, in one of the most publicised crimes of Maroubra Beach, was shot in the head by one of his mates (who was my mate too) in a drug-fuelled explosion. His body was then thrown into the sea. Many said that

Troy got what he deserved, being a convicted stand-over man, rapist and God-only knew what else. But that entire case was quite heavy. Sam died mysteriously, while on some drug with a group of dodgy friends in Bali. His body was dumped at a tip. Terry killed himself because his girlfriend left him for another guy. An ex-girlfriend was run over and killed. She was drunk and arguing with her new boyfriend in the middle of a busy road.

Others were luckier. Karl recovered from the Day Club shooting and Brad lost an eye during a stabbing in the city. Assaults, stabbings and shootings seemed to sporadically continue on. There were too many going down — dying from car accidents while drunk, or simply dropping dead in their thirties. Many others were 'lucky' enough to end up in a concrete jail cell, rather than a wooden tomb. Reg got ten years in LA County prison for trying to smuggle cocaine onto a flight. Brett and Alex were both caught taking pot to a surf camp in Indonesia and did six months of brutal fight-or-fall time in a remote Sumatran prison. They spent each day watching each other's back, continually getting into fights with the other prisoners because they were foreigners.

Everyone had a sorry story to tell — divorces and affairs, and charges of driving under the influence of alcohol, drugs, assault, fraud — even murder. Some lost their businesses because of drug addictions. Many just phlegmatically floated around, obviously burnt out and spat out from the scene. They signed off from society with new do-not-disturb personalities, because disturbed they had become, with complex pharmaceutical words now tattooed to their memory. One friend had mastered the art of mixing alcohol and cocaine with certain pharmaceutical prescriptions his doctor had given him for his new mental disorder. Countless more unceremoniously departed from the city to try and find some type of peace in the countryside, too fragile to endure the pain of living near anyone or anything that pushed too many sensitive buttons. And those who were left, well normality was for everyone to be coming down mid-week, every week, from drugs and/or alcohol, which supported the excuse for being ignorant, shitty and drawing on whatever negative superlatives one could muster. Normality *was* drugs. Life *was* Sex, Drugs and Techno.

The numbers were grim, but I kept up a fake facade of stoicism, even though I felt I was starting to lose *my* resilient edge. I could tell everyone was becoming as deeply fragile as me. I could see it in their eyes. Our childhood bonds didn't seem so relevant anymore and the pseudo-bond of ecstasy and the club scene could no longer ignite our journeys of the past. Drugs began to play out the opposite effect of distortion, distrust and disunity. Everyone was spinning erratically around the Sex, Drugs and Techno scene. I couldn't stand the messed-up state that they were all in, yet I arrogantly denied being so out of touch myself. I continued to become so engulfed in my own spiralling world that I really didn't care what news I heard from anyone, whether good or bad. I didn't care if I heard from anyone at all. Anyone!

There was no room for reflection. Sex, Drugs and Techno had me. It had us all. Pushing the body was a gallant weekly trophy, an accepted sign of one's social bravado. If we did all get together, once the beers served as entrees, the lines of cocaine would always follow, again artificially solidifying our childhood bonds and camaraderie. All of us 'locked-up' with quivering lips, talking shit — again — till all hours of the morning. Who would be the last man standing?

To say no to a beer, a line, or to even leave early, would bring on a barrage from all around me. Too often, I simply went for a pee and snuck out just to get home — even at eight in the morning, mid-week. I remember one morning back at a friend's place, after a night out, the boys wouldn't let Johnno leave, urging him to push on. So he went to the bathroom, climbed out the window and scaled down three floors, using the old external plumbing pipes as footing. My friends had a loyal trait. They are the type of guys you would want to have around you in the heat of a battle. If you were in trouble, everyone would be there to help. And when you were partying, that staunch support was just as strong — everyone would be there to push you on.

12. A time to reflect

I MET A YOUNG WOMAN named Renee at a friend's birthday dinner. Renee had a beautiful presence. She was sweet, well-spoken and genuinely interested in me. She didn't have that washed out, drug-hungry clubber look like most women I ended up with for one-night-stands. We found a connection and throughout the evening I showed her the respect she deserved. She somehow tamed the sleazy persona I was now conquering women with. Our evening was spent chatting and finding a chemistry. I was filled with a new sense of aliveness. We arranged to meet over the weekend and went for lunch, returning to her place afterwards.

We relaxed on her sofa and to feel her close to me was quite moving — and anxious. I felt that this may be a chance to change course with a woman who wasn't hung up in the Sex, Drugs and Techno scene. I realised that I couldn't find the courage to move closer; intimacy was somewhat uncomfortable for me. In the past, with sex — and drugs and alcohol — the motivating impetus, I made my moves with the confidence of a man who knew how to get what he wanted. But now I felt vulnerable and unworthy of this precious gift that lay before me. She must have felt this, and she guided her long brown fringe behind her ear, moved closer and kissed me. It was ever so tender. I didn't want this to be just like all the others and I let the moment move freely to whichever way it was meant to go. Eventually, we made what felt like love, my mind for once totally absorbed with the woman held in my arms. That energy of gratuitous sex was subdued. There was no rush, no urge to conquer or achieve. I was in the moment — with her, in that special moment.

Afterwards, as I lay on the bed she took a shower and I daydreamed off to an exciting relationship that may have just begun. After what seemed like quite a long time for a shower, I went to the door and asked if she was okay. There was no response. Again I asked, but still no response. I cautiously opened the bathroom door and went closer to the shower. Concerned now, I looked behind the shower curtain and she was sitting on the floor of the recess with the water running over her, curled up with her face resting on her knees. I went to her side and held her, asking what was wrong. I noticed she was crying and her face was filled with sadness. She wouldn't answer me. I turned off the shower, grabbed a towel and wrapped it around her, quite stunned by what was taking place.

Consoling her in the best way I could without knowing what was wrong, we sat on the sofa and I said, 'If I can help you in any way I will. If you feel in some way I haven't treated you with respect, I'm sorry.' I didn't know what was wrong or what to say, or if I had done something or said something. I had no idea what was wrong. Finally, she looked at me. 'Paul, you are the first guy... I mean, I've felt something since being with you that I haven't felt ever before,' her words difficult to get out. 'But these feelings have stirred up some things inside of me that have been buried for a long time.' She began to cry again as I held her in my arms.

'It's okay, you don't have to tell me if you feel you can't. Don't worry, right now we have each other and I'm here for you.' I could feel her pain.

She looked into my eyes again, seemingly wanting to share her angst with me. I could see that she was trying, but couldn't find the strength or words to convey her pain.

'It's okay. It's okay.' My hugs, I hoped, were sending her the empathy I was feeling.

After a pause, she composed herself and said, 'I need to go back to my parents' home for a couple of days, just to think a bit. They live two hours by train up the coast and if you could take me to the train station that would be really helpful.'

'Whatever it is you need, I'd be happy to do.'

'I'm so sorry about this,' she whispered.

'Don't be sorry. Whatever it is you are feeling will be okay.' She hugged me and I didn't want to let her go. She had touched a deep chord within me.

The trip to the train station was quiet but not at all tense. She again apologised for what had happened and said that she would be ready to tell me when she returned. 'If I haven't scared you off,' her smile lighting up her sweet face.

It was a nice change of atmosphere and I returned the same lightness with, 'Well, I have quite a past. It probably should have been me in the shower.'

She laughed and placed her hand on my shoulder and said, 'Thanks, Paul. I appreciate your sweetness so much.' The mood had definitely shifted and with another smile she said, 'Maybe I'll end up back in the shower if you tell me all about your past.'

'When the time is right, I'd like to share with you my journey,' I said, more seriously. 'Let's not worry about anything — *anything*. Whatever the problems are, they can be overcome, yours and mine. We'll overcome everything. Don't worry,' I confidently replied.

It was a beautiful calming of what had taken place. As her train was departing, she said she would call me in a few days. She said she would let me know when she was arriving back in town and I could come and pick her up. Our parting smiles were consoling, and the final sparkle in our eyes was enough for us both to hold that special something we had captured.

Over the next couple of days, I couldn't get Renee out of my thoughts. I reminisced every beautiful moment, from our first introduction to making love. Renee somehow broke through my self-protective layer of romance — even commitment. She was special. She was different. I was filled with hope, excitement and the beginning of a new chapter in my life.

It had been four days since she left town and as I only had her home phone number I had no way of contacting her at her parents' place. I began to connect to the negative thoughts of maybe it was me who brought on her sadness — that she no longer wanted to see me. Or perhaps my joke about me ending up in the shower was a bit insensitive. Then I received an unexpected phone call from a woman whose voice was fraught with grief.

'Is this Paul?'

'Yes, who's speaking?'

'I'm Renee's sister, Julie.' She began to cry. I felt a tenseness start to grip at my chest.

'Paul, I am so sorry to tell you this. Renee has taken her life.' I broke down, feeling that surging jolt tear into my heart, just like when I heard Dad had died. It was a feeling I hoped I would never feel again. We both sobbed for what seemed like an eternity.

'What happened?' my voice croaking and breaths shallow.

After a long pause, she continued, 'Paul, Renee never stopped talking about you after she arrived home. She told me what happened in the shower and she was so moved by the way you cared for her — she was totally moved by you. As far as I knew she was going back to Sydney to share with you why that happened, but then...' Again, her crying brought me to my knees. 'But then, two days ago, we all went out for the day and Renee was at home on her own. When we returned...' She cried and cried. I cried and cried and cried. My heart was aching. I didn't even know the person I was speaking with, but I felt we were one in that tragic moment. We both were filled with the sadness that was the loss of such a beautiful human being.

'We found her in the garage. She hanged herself. There was nothing anyone could do. We were too late.' Then there was silence — numb silence. 'Paul, I wanted to let you know that this had nothing to do with you. It was not your fault. Renee was hurt as a child and she never got over it. We just didn't realise how much pain she still carried inside.'

'Julie, if you don't mind me asking, what happened to Renee?'

'Not at all, I wanted to tell you. When Renee was twelve, she was raped by her uncle and his wife. She told our parents but they never believed her because the wife turned the entire allegation back onto Renee's troublemaking. Consequently, the rapes continued till she was fourteen. No one believed her, so she just endured it all. I suppose back then it was different — everyone thought that sort of thing just didn't happen. She kept the pain of it all buried for so long. When she met someone who she felt something special with for the first time, it was all too much.'

I had lost many friends to the fast lane, even from suicide and never once did I feel any deep remorse. Saddened shock, yes, but we all took the risks and pushed it to the limits head on. The demise of my friends was an expected outcome. They fell as they lived — fast. But Renee was innocent. She *was* a victim. She had no control over her pain. Anger and sadness filled every cell of my tarnished body, and my mind surged with thoughts of how fucked life is and how fucked up I was. My sad journey of glitz, glamour and garbage was not to alter course in the arms of Renee. My lonely and lost life had to carry on to see what card the overseer of my life would deal me next.

13. The real lonely planet

I WAS IN A CITY PUB one morning after another all-night binge, looking at an old man slumped at the end of the bar, alone and withered. He numbly sat there with a blank stare. The pub was his lifeline. I thought to myself, *Where did it all go wrong for* **him?** *I* was needlessly turning into a new-age millennium loner. I was becoming that man in the bar. I had turned onto the wrong path, missed the warning signs and ended up travelling along towards the fast lane. What a mess. I would look into the eyes of others and they would look into mine, each trying to emit that tower of strength and clarity that was once our birthright. But I would know; they would know — though it was a tightly guarded topic. I pushed society and society pushed me. There were no winners. Forget about mid-life crisis at forty. Mine was alive and kicking back in my twenties, masked with an 'it'll be right' attitude.

Things had changed. I had changed. My friends had changed and so had the scene. I didn't know who I was anymore. Was that me, with my arms around my mates, yahooing with a belly full of alcohol, or with a head full of coke raving into someone's ear, or with that girl in a passionate embrace in the middle of the dance floor with my body full of E? Or was I really how I felt most of the time now — a total mess? I could vaguely recall a time when life seemed so much more real. I had lost the person I was as a teenager — optimistic, dynamic and vibrant. I remember school, being full of enthusiasm, ready to take on and change the world. Well I certainly changed my own inner world. In the beginning, drugs seemed more innocent and fun and I only had to weather a day or two to be ready to kick start another weekend at full throttle. My body felt sound, having plenty of reserves of stamina and spirit to recuperate and keep up the pace, and my mind's agitation abated without any lasting —

obvious — turmoil. I felt fine eventually, so why not, was the robust call from within, lapsing the memory of an otherwise abortive week.

But now, after some twenty years of consuming drugs and alcohol, what was in the beginning only a couple of fragile days now began to span the entire week. It was ongoing as the caustic muck was sinking deeper into my system and staying there — physically, mentally and emotionally. I was no novice anymore and while everyone was saying that the pills were better five to ten years earlier, I was becoming a toxic waste dump and my body was tired. 'I'm fine' were nothing more than empty words. People knew the real me by looking at my teary eyes and shaky lips. Partying had altered my entire life, a life that was continuing to build in intensity but was going nowhere but down. Everyone else had their own inner turmoil, obvious from their shitty comedowns and weird behaviour that couldn't be shared, let alone controlled and comprehended. It was push on, keep my mouth shut and try and act as if I was still strong.

The smell of alcohol-stained carpets and stale smoke began to repulse me. My joy and love of music and DJing was diminishing. It was interwoven with my social life and separating work from play became impossible. Even playing drug and alcohol free couldn't protect me from that seductive and intense environment. My job was to induce that energy with my music. During the week I was trying to pull it all together and freshen up, while continually looking for more new transcendent music to buy. That kept a kind of hypnotic pulse flowing through me, constantly and subliminally holding me in orbit of the scene and all of its force. And if I did begin to feel a bit of clarity, it was short-lived. I dragged myself into the club at two in the morning and wrapped myself in work and *that* environment. Free vodkas, or whatever, would keep it all moving the way it was meant to be.

Women went from giving me enticing gestures to staying clear, as I began to give off some sort of unpleasant energy. I began to act like a desperate manic, mechanically seducing any woman who would want to connect to my predatory, sleazy moves. And those who did stumble into my latching arms I was sure were as lost and empty as I. My first blissful ecstasy experiences were now a distant blur. The love drug was turning on me. I was finally starting to understand why those rehab celebrities eventually say, *NO TO DRUGS!* And I also understood how many ended up back on the same path.

Time became a blur. *Where did Monday go? When will the comedown pass? What time is it? How long has this circus been going?* Life became a mish-mash. It was a mess!

Even the sanctity of my home changed dramatically. The big city was continuing to develop high-rise unit blocks that made me feel like a penned-in battery cage hen, confining me to my four walls. I felt so close to it all, but yet so far from everything. I read that a New York study found that people who lived in high-rise apartments were more likely to suffer from anxiety. Throw drugs into the mix and there's a good dosage of fear. As I looked around town at all those new concrete boxes stacked on top of each other, called homes, I would wonder if any of those new tenants would get the chance to engage and interact with their neighbours.

For me, the only chance to catch up with the people living around me was in the lift. Every day, that tiny little space of interactive opportunity would be full of people wearing their sunglasses and those without would not give me any eye contact — except the elderly people, funnily enough! The silence was deafening and, as the lift doors opened onto ground zero, the relieving surge was like removing a plastic bag from over my head after sixty seconds. Growing up, I had become used to running across to my neighbour's yard for a chat, but this had now transformed to become a robotic placement in a coffin called a lift, with an engaging exchange declining into nothing more than a lacklustre sideways lift of the lip.

And outside my front door, the grandeur of my cosmopolitan metropolis awaited, with the heroin-addicted prostitutes, numbed-out like mannequins, propped up on the corner. The smell of urine and faeces wafted from the car park exit door — tokens of gratitude to society from the numerous derelict, homeless alcoholics who sat across the road in their own discon-nected yet harmonious packs, blending into the cityscape. City living certainly did give me the world at my feet. But what world was I now in?

14. Dr Feelgood

WHILE I SPENT MY TWENTIES trying to lose myself, by the time I tried to magically feel *me* again it was too late. The horse had bolted. I didn't know where to go or what to do. I had developed an insatiable appetite for understanding the power of ecstasy, but it had led to somewhere in total polarity to what I believed it to be. *Why? How? Maybe it's just me? Maybe I'm just a weak, crazy loser? No! Something is happening and I need to find out what it is.* I was sure that the warped information narcotics exposed me to needed complete understanding if I were to totally regain my zest for life, but I could not understand nor discover the truth behind this bizarre world. My mind continued to question the unreal, but there were more critical issues to deal with other than understanding what seemed like a lot of hocus-pocus.

I sought treatments to assist my flailing body. I visited holistic therapists, seeking treatments that would regulate my consti-pated bowels, clean my furry tongue, dry out my chronic phlegm, unlock my atrophied back, relieve my daily migraines, calm my paranoid episodes, and so on. I tried numerous diets of abstinence of certain foods and choosing specific food groups, such as low GI, high protein, non-dairy, vegetarian, all of which failed to work. I tried osteopathy, massage, acupuncture, yoga, Qigong, kung fu, kundalini tantra, Bowen, reiki, colonic irrigation, holistic counselling, Satsung — even tarot and palm reading. I was hoping someone would have the magic key to pull me back together, yet no one did. Some of these I embraced for a period, others just once, simply wanting someone to understand my pain with an open ear. I found that these alternative method-ologies were powerful in their own right, and I did gain some useful information. Yet relative to drugs and my dark state, none of those practitioners could offer me anything other than I was out of balance of each particular practice. That was for sure!

I even stooped to getting erotic massages every now and then, with an erroneous attitude of having all my issues addressed at once — the soothing and caring hands of a woman, pain relief, and a sexual release at the end of the treatment via masturbation. I wanted and needed so many things, but everywhere I turned was continual pain, attachments, desires and weakness, and the massage parlour gave me momentary peace at the end of one of those erotic sessions. That's what I was looking for — peace. In some bizarre way, having an orgasm offered me the abatement of my torment. Holistic treatments made me feel relaxed and at ease with my physical pain, but an erotic encounter at the massage parlour felt like a total appeasement of that force working through me. It was total peace at the end, like the monster had been put to rest — until it returned later. I wanted peace, yet some force was driving me, consuming me and wanting gratification. Without any breakthrough, my vehicle of life was breaking down, and so frustration took me back to the familiar — DJing, clubs, partying, drugs and alcohol. This led me back to the same, sorry cycle — weakness, anxiousness, pain and depressive boredom. Continually lamenting, *I really am over all of this bullshit,* my mind's constant mantra for months on end was, *I can't do this anymore,* and its scathing judgment, *You're fucked!*

I couldn't deny the fact anymore. Hiding from people, on-edge and uncomfortable when around people, a body clogged up — it was there every day now and it wasn't budging. *Just walk away from it all, Paul.* Somehow, it kept a hold of me. At times, I fought back and joyously thought, *Wow, great, it's been about two months since I took anything bad, did anything stupid.* Then wham — frustration, inner torment, and some empty belief that I needed to feel alive in my hollow life, had me cave in down the fast lane again. The truth was inescapable, but I wasn't ready to fully accept it. So another day, another week would start with me at the bottom of an ever-growing pile of broken dreams. I felt as if I was in suspended animation, and the need to feel good — *somehow* — was overwhelming. The club scene was the only domain I knew of where I could get some kind of prolonged release from my daily struggle with reality, and so back I went. Many times I didn't want to leave the club, for I knew that when I did, reality was there waiting. As time went on, it all became increasingly familiar, and increasingly tragic. I was living the consequences of what I had created. Life as I knew it had become stale, empty and a lost journey. It was pure ground hog day, over and over again. Hope I Get Help — *HIGH* — became an acronym for me.

Under duress, I decided to visit a doctor. He diagnosed acute anxiety disorder. He advised some medication and said that, with my symptoms and history of drug use, I may have to take medication for life. Succumbing to such a finale was a crushing blow. *Medication! I have totally failed.* I went to see another doctor and it was exactly the same diagnosis and cure. It was the first time I felt my future's options were limited. All I wanted now was peace and the doctor wanted to give me more pills — *legal* stimulants — possibly for life.

'Take one tablet in the morning and one at night — and don't take on an empty stomach' was not the way I wanted to come out the other side, in some spurious state of feeling alive. With pen in hand, ready to scribble out a prescription like a sportsman signing autographs, somehow remaining totally detached from me, I declined both doctors' advice that my hopes of regaining my health without medication, with my history, were fruitless. But medication was not to be the option. It was a deep conviction. What was, I had no idea.

15. Where am I?

THE WARMTH OF THE SUNSET began to feel like a torchlight blaring into my eyes at night and the singing birds vying for slumber positions within the trees outside drew my senses back into the reality of what was left of the remainder of the day. The room was unfamiliar. I painfully pushed myself across the bed and out of the sunlight. A few moments were needed to first scan through the mental checklist of how my body was faring. To feel the fragility of my entire being was a deflating moment, which triggered my mind into a numb, bitter thought: *Why did I do it?* Every part of me was drained and shaky and, for a moment, I simply wanted to close my eyes again and wish the moment away.

Too many times now, I had endured this post-nightclub feeling and today was becoming all too familiar. My mind began to move forward and visualise the week that awaited me. My breaths were shallow. It felt like any sudden jolt would send me off to meet my maker, such was the all-over weakness of my body. I could not stop thinking of how disappointed I was with myself and with the week that lay in store for me, a thought that deflated any hope of a lift in spirit.

I was trying to work out exactly where I was. I was naked in a double bed. The room was neat with a set of drawers topped with the standard plethora of beauty accessories of which men will never truly comprehend their uses. There was a side table and chair, with my clothes folded neatly over the backrest. There was a walk-in mirrored wardrobe, in which I could see a reflection of a large, tropical photograph hanging from the wall above the bed. The photograph held my gaze, allowing my mind a moment to float off with the palm trees and white sandy beach. I was thinking of Bali and my trips there surfing the cleansing waves of Uluwatu. *Ah... Bali,* I thought. Upon the side table was a clock, which read 6:15 p.m. There was no noise coming from outside the bedroom and I lay there for another twenty minutes. *Another big night; another one-night-stand.* Lethargically, I found the strength to rise to my rickety feet.

My clothes were drenched with a pungent smell of stale smoke, now the signature scent for me, and putting them on really felt like another slap in the face. I really didn't care where I was; I just wanted to get home and soak in my hot bath. Walking out from the bedroom, at my feet was a piece of paper laid out on the floor. I picked it up. It read: 'Hope you are feeling okay. Will be back at nine with some food. Hope you will stay.' The name was forgotten as soon as I read it. Staying was not an option and I walked back into the room, first checking to see if all my personals were still with me. I grabbed my shoes. The soles were caked with the now-accustomed gum, cigarette butts and God knows what else. A quick look in the mirror brought on another self-critical thought, as my whole face resembled my shoes. My eyes were bloodshot, one half-closed, one fully pinned; my skin was paste-like and I had a lost look that gave off nothing more than doll's eye fixation. I made Ozzy Osbourne look like a beacon of health. With my fouled clothes clinging to me like a cumbersome reminder of the night before, I left the apartment knowing that another woman was being left with a justified reminder as to why many men are viewed as bastards. Walking out into the twilight, I sought to gain some bearing on my location. It was suburbia. That's all I knew.

I walked up to the main road and waited for a taxi, which took a couple of minutes but it seemed like an eternity. As I relaxed into the back seat, the driver looked at me through the rear-view mirror, asking where I wanted to go. I told him to take me to paradise, and then apologised and gave him my address. The driver, a small Asian man, turned and looked very intently at me and said in polite, soft broken English, 'Sir, me can take you to your address, but you want to go to paradise, you already there. Is inside you.'

He turned back and drove the cab, not saying another word.

Pulling into my unit, I handed him the money and as he prepared my change he looked at me and said, 'Sir, you find paradise.' It was the warmest experience of the weekend. As I alighted from the cab, the street girls were busy on the corner waiting to fall into a passing car. Sex was littered all across the city. There was a smorgasbord out there, whether you paid for it, or hunted it — and I had heartburn. I was just as tarred as those girls hanging out on my corner. We were all desperate.

What I really wanted then in that moment was sugar, like some opiate drug squeezing me tighter. I was now craving sugar foods every day and, after a big night, it was a matter of urgency. The urge for sex came and went, easily appeased with the seductive club scene or the occasional massage, but sugar meant the difference between peace and excruciating pain — daily. I knew it would exacerbate my now-chronic anxiety, but it crept up on me ever so subtly. Before I became aware of it, I found myself gorging any food made with sugar. Again, that momentary space of peace was now an automated act of relief. With a cap and sunglasses, I would anxiously enter shops and order enough treats for a party, making lame excuses, like it was for a dinner party, or the family. One day, the surly girl behind the counter just looked at me and said, 'Yeah, right!' Most times, I never made it home. I just sat in my car or stood in the street and stuffed it in.

And today was no different. I hurried down to the corner store to buy all sorts of treats. I couldn't get home quick enough to gorge it all, then lock myself away from society. Chocolates, biscuits and breakfast cereal — I ingested it all till I was sick. Some monster inside had been completely appeased. The weekend was now complete. I was at peace. The torment was gone.

After a long hot bath, my thoughts began teasing me once again about the coming week and then sinking deeper into the way my life was playing out — my job, my socialising, my life. I knew I was faltering. I was going down for the count. My job was the scene, familiarity was the scene and the scene had become my enemy. And now, I was addicted to sugar... but life was far from sweet.

16. The final curtain

IT WAS 4 A.M. ONE SUNDAY MORNING and I was playing at the leading club in Jakarta between playing in Bali. The whole scene of music, parties, drugs and every bit of physical and emotional baggage that tags along for the ride was becoming too much to bear. My ego didn't give a damn if I sounded like a star or a bum buskin' the streets, such was the inner turmoil engulfing my world. All I was consumed with was my fantasy of a better life. I was ready to simply take off one day, never to return. I felt that that day was near.

The club, which I had never been to before but heard that it was a *serious* venue, was downtown. At four in the morning it looked like Grand Central Station at rush hour. The place was teeming with people outside and my minder proudly excelled in pointing out the finer attributes of his palace.

'It opens at Friday sunset and stays open till Monday afternoon — non-stop. It has four floors and you will be playing in the main arena. We have a floor for patrons to shower and refresh, a floor dedicated to prostitutes and numerous restaurants. There are three music rooms. You have pumping music, ya?'

Ambling into the prodigious citadel I could immediately sense that *it was* a serious venue. It was the new millennium's global odyssey for the young and free, and I was the next maestro of the night, though deep down I felt that I was nearing my *coup de grace. Could this be my swansong?* Seeing the gaunt, ghost-like faces walking out past me was like looking into a mirror. I saw the same lost sadness in everyone's pinned, fractured eyes. The place was a catacomb, with a matrix of corridors, a rumbling beat in the distance and that familiar nightclub smell, which instantly loosened my tender stomach. I detoured to the nearest toilet, sitting there in the lingering stench with my feet wallowing within the now-accustomed soaking toilet paper that littered the floor around me, thinking to myself, *What the hell am I doing here?*

The hosts, as always, were forthcoming with whatever I needed for the night — *anything* I wanted. I knew how fragile I was and opted for water, which brought on a look of disbelief. *This old DJ just wants water!* As I entered the main arena I could not believe what I saw. I had been to some of the finest clubs in the world and some, very dark-themed, but this place began to answer many of my questions. The moment I walked into this space, certain things finally made sense. Something clicked inside. I was ready to finally see the underlying energy that pulsated within those walls of darkness.

The club's decor was designed with serpents' heads, ghoulish figures and bizarre, bestial statuettes, which pierced the high walls between the mezzanine terraces that were packed with the rolling hips of hard-core revellers. Gazing towards the heavens, the roof was oozing with voluminous contorted imagery, as the striking, tangled laser lights caught the collective, reflective pseudo-sparkle in the eyes of the crowd. The club exuded a miry, barren vibration like it was pulled straight out of a Bram Stoker story.

As I stood there in awe, a tap on my shoulder had me turn to be accosted by an aging woman who placed her mouth to my ear and softly whispered, 'You want lady?' I looked to where she was pointing. Sitting on the sofas were a dozen or so seductive 'ladies', all giving *that* look. Before I had the chance to let the demons fill my thoughts, my minder interjected and led me through the crowd to the DJ booth.

I was in another world. I began to feel exhilaration churn from within me as I eagerly anticipated placing my hands upon the turntables. I was in DJ nirvana. Suddenly overcome with a deep euphoria, this club was drawing me in and lifting me up. The rock star feeling returned, churning from within. With my hands shuffling through my prized vinyl collection, I searched for an opening track that would gravitate us all towards our destination as quickly as possible — though most in the cauldron were already there. It was I who wanted to unite with them, to reinstate that perpetual state of purgatory. A final beholding, visual sweep across the room caught glimpses of lust, hatred and numbness, spewing out from the zombie-like stares transfixed upon me throughout the crowd. I was ready to go all the way with this rite of passage.

A few songs into my set, a tender stroke on my arm presented a stunning, tall woman who said, 'Beautiful music.' She then placed her long index finger and thumb into my mouth like a smiling assassin, placing a pill onto my tongue and then sliding her finger seductively back out and down over my chin. My defences crumbled, my pain and angst now a distant nightmare as I surrendered and opened my fragile system, accepting the virulent 'apple' and all that she and that place represented. I wanted that moment and was going to divulge all and be swept away as if there were no tomorrow. I was one with all before me as I played on, conveying the signature of my tarnished, barren soul through the music and out into the crowd, with that blissful fuzziness, once again opening me up to call upon the ardour of the effigies looking ominously over me. I was riding that wave once again, as I turned to my minder and requested a double vodka, soda and fresh lemon in a long glass. He lit up and hastily threw an order at one of his staff, eager to get me whatever it was to keep the place floating over the rhythmical edge of the never-never. This was more than entertainment. This was soul-wrenching levitation and I clicked with the crowd as we celebrated the forces at hand like some medieval ritual. The snake of darkness had arrived, declaring its intent to defile my soul.

Faces on the dance floor were melting into a grotesque, laughing freak show and, through the jigsaw of strobes, visions of demons pierced my peripheral vision. The crowd danced on as I joined forces with them in an orgasm of trance, all riding this rush of our reality they call a night out and I called my job. I melted into the madness, eager to grab track after track and act like the Pied Piper, leading us all deeper into the twilight zone, with my music a catalytic series of hymns, guiding us deeper through the Grim Reaper's gateway, which we had all entered long before this night.

Upon the commencement of the next DJ, I walked through the crowd and I came crashing down almost in an instant. I sat in the shadows, away from the crowd and the lights, like a deviant hiding in some subway corner, and literally felt my entire being ready to crack. I just wanted to close my eyes and wake up in another life, far from this club, this city and this madness. Reflection was an understatement. My stark and crucifying reality returned once again, a crude and progressive reminder of just what state my life was in. Being in an unfamiliar town, feeling isolated from my comfort zone, my fragility felt ten-fold. It was time to accept that I was nothing more than a weak, immature man who fell in love with the drug scene with a gluttonous desire and who used my music passion and talent for my own self-serving needs. The skin over my cheekbones sagged further into my dry, clammy mouth and the gum I had been chewing for half the night was the perfect metaphor for me — I was gnawed-up beyond repair and I should have been spat out long ago. I had to endure another on-edge sleepless night. I was scared. Something felt ready and about to give way.

Why was it that in my moment of madness, surrendering and accepting another pill turned *this* performance into one of the most powerful gigs I had experienced? It was probably not what I wanted to believe, nor fathom, but I knew deep down in the distant mist of my tiring spirit that I had finally pushed it to the ultimate limit within the realms of sanity. For years I had blindly followed where drugs led me. I had now tasted the real 'ecstasy' of pure darkness and all of the fun and loose freedom I had been engaging in over the years was simply grooming me for that moment when it would all click together — tonight. I entered *somewhere* as this force gave me what it knew would satiate me into submission in my weakened state — Sex, Drugs and Techno. Some channel into the darker domain of life was now tormenting me. This energy seemed fostered and powerful enough to show its abdicating mask unabated, determined to consume me in a way that reached beyond the boundaries of medical science. Where to go from here was anyone's guess. I wasn't sure whether to call a doctor, my Mum, or a priest.

My journey back to Bali from Jakarta was a nightmare. Jakarta's air was as rancid as any nightclub's at seven in the morning. I gasped for any type of cleanliness, yet it was nowhere to be found — in neither the environment nor me. The shanty-like streets on the outskirts of the city were scattered with people with the worst deformities I have ever seen, their luckless birthrights freaking me out like a lingering residue from my demonic episodes the night before. At the airport I must have looked like some dodgy smack smuggler more akin to Bangkok. It was the worst I had ever felt, and in a country where *everyone* stops and stares at you, my paranoia was beyond overwhelming.

Arriving back in Bali, there was a slight sense of respite. The general sweetness and softness of the Balinese was consoling. The entire Bali experience touched me deeply. Every time I set foot onto its volcanic landscape, I reserved the highest regard for the respect that its people show to themselves, their community and visitors. But I had a major dance party to play that night and I wasn't sure how I was going to cope, let alone turn up. But I had to — I had to turn up and I had to cope. I locked myself in my hotel room dreading the setting of the sun, for I knew that it was going to be a very long and difficult night. I lay in my bed and stared at the walls till 3:30 a.m. CNN played the problems of the world to me over and over — keeping me in good company. Unable to catch any sleep due to my abhorrent mind racing non-stop, and with no sleep the drug-induced night before, I was redlining in overdrive. At 4 a.m. a driver picked me up and I made it to the gig.

The party itself was amazing — an open air venue at a cliff-top resort on the island's Bukit peninsula. The glamorous had come from all over the world, but I didn't want any part of it. The beautiful looked ugly and dirty, the fun a sad illusion and I was beyond insipid. At 5 a.m. I began my set. The dance floor was completely packed with the party in full swing. Taking over from the other DJ, my opening track was progressing and I turned away from the crowd to choose the next one, my records stacked behind me. On turning back to the crowd, I couldn't believe it. The dance floor was almost completely empty. I thought, *Oh no! I've scared them all off.* Gobsmacked, I focused and saw that a tropical thunderstorm had arrived just at that moment. It poured torrentially. I played on to an empty dance floor, again thinking, *What the hell am I doing here?* I played for another hour, but the now-drizzling rain continued, holding off the crowd from returning to the dance floor. With the crowd all but gone, the organiser decided to end the party an hour early and that was it. The plug was pulled. DJing and drugs were no more for me. Some twenty years of drugs and ten years of DJing, the ride had run out of steam. I was as washed out as that party.

I'd always known of the mystical power of Bali and I believed that I got a taste of it that night. The way the rain fell like it did precisely at the moment I started was for me a strong message — enough is enough. The dance floor was empty because I was empty. I had nothing more to give. As I was driven back into town, the clouds parted and the sacred Mount Agung rose majestically in the distance. It was the most consoling moment of the past few days.

Part Two

17. Island of the Gods

MY EARLY EXPERIENCES ON ECSTASY had left me with one defining legacy that I continued to hold in awe. Ecstasy has immense power — individually and collectively — to open the heart. Experiencing what I honestly believed to be the true power of the heart, real brotherly love and feeling connected to all and everything around me, ecstasy *had* to have more relevance than a bit of chalk the size of a pea. That explosive reaction triggered some biblical universal essence, parting the clouds of my conditioned upbringing. I (an entire generation) believed I tasted where our evolution is meant to shine.

The more I tried to grasp at that essence through ecstasy, the more it drifted away, to be replaced with the darker aspects of the human form, with an eventual realisation that drugs are not the answer to life's meaning. And so a seed of spiritual disenchantment churned away in the shadows within for a long time — that 'something missing' cliché. The ultimate prize in this life, my Holy Grail of the heart, had me languishing for a transcendent ideal, yearning for my predestined fate. I believed ecstasy was a doorway to the heavens, but couldn't understand why the experience ended in pain and misery. I often lay in my bed hungry to discover the true connection between heart and heaven, without drugs.

Back in my Kuta hotel, it was time to chill out. I needed something pretty amazing to pull me out of this mess. I planned an extra week on the island before returning to Australia, but wasn't sure if I even had the emotional strength to leave my hotel room. I certainly didn't have the strength to go back to Australia. Home conjured up instant fear and pain. I needed to get away from the tourist/party scene of Kuta, but wasn't sure where to go. It was then that I remembered a practitioner in Australia mentioning an unorthodox healer, named Ratu Bagus, located at the foot of Mount Agung. He wasn't advertised anywhere or widely known, only that his ashram was close to the temples near the foot of the volcano. My curiosity was aroused and a burning desire filled me to seek out this place. I thought that type of person — especially in Bali — might serve me well in my state.

After a couple of days of sleep and lying by the pool, I hired a car and driver and headed for the cloud-draped highlands, determined to uncover this mystery that my mind excited itself with. On a deeper level, I felt that if there was a place here that could share the wisdom and secrets of its people, I was ready to lay my soul bare. We spent the day traversing the pot-tainted roads as the intermittent smell of earthen patchouli drifted from the jungle. Stopping and asking at villages, we received blank looks, though the smiling chants of 'Halo Mista' from the children were as quenching as the cool water I drank to ward off the tropical heat. The countryside of Bali, away from the Western-tainted club scene of Kuta, was a refreshing experience. People laughed in the streets, waving graciously as we drove by, intrigued by the visitor passing their way. Finally, as the shadows began to draw longer, we found this modest Balinese Shangri-La perched above a flowing stream, surrounded by rice paddies and jungle, with the majestic Mount Agung towering in the near distance.

I waved goodbye to my driver and as I entered through the old bamboo gates I could see movement and hear numerous painful screams coming from the old wooden structure nearby. A sweet Balinese woman greeted me with a cup of tea and a warm smile. She had the face of an angel and her sincerity was touching. Her name was Ketut. My curiosity was drawn to the *taman,* as she proudly called it, and the strange activity happening inside.

'Would you like to shake now?' she asked. I was eager to experience the knowledge of this surreptitious place, though *shaking* did not quite register with me.

Walking through the doorway of the taman, I was in no way prepared for what I was about to witness. The old, rustic room, as raw as the jungle around us, was filled with an array of elegant, eclectic wooden statues and carvings, some of which depicted demonic forms that triggered my association to similar effigies in that Jakarta club. An array of vibrant colour from the many food offerings to the Gods lay beautifully designed on hand-carved pedestals and the walls were draped with authentic tribal art. The smell of sweet incense filled the air.

I stood there with a confused look as I witnessed ten or so Western people and about twenty Balinese standing on the spot, shaking their bodies to music playing, not in a type of dynamic dance rhythm, but simply standing firm, pulsating their movements in a repetitive, grounding flow, much like riding an imaginary horse. Their stance and focus were directed to the front of the taman, where sitting upon a thrown-like wooden chair was a resounding man, with long black hair pulled back, clad beautifully in a toga-like white gown. He was piercing an eagle-eye stare back towards the shakers, in what looked like the engagement of a serious practice. The lights in the taman were casting a reflective lustre upon his broad forehead, which was smooth and shiny, like he'd never had a worry in the world. The Westerners were sweating profusely, with some retching in pain and wallowing out constant screams and convulsions. Numerous chickens pecked at the cracked, cement floor beneath their feet. The chickens were then chased by the unusually healthy (for Bali) ashram dogs.

The man sitting down turned his focus to me and his stern face immediately lit up with the smile of a long lost friend, warm and genuinely happy to see me. He walked up to me and with a resonant 'Hello,' he placed both arms around me and pulled me into his bulking frame, hugging me with a warmth I had not experienced ever before. In that moment I wanted to just cry in his arms. He let go and took hold of my wrist, leading me closer to the others. Before I had a chance to introduce myself, let alone chat, his face went back to a serious demeanour and he said in broken English, 'You focus on Ratu picture! You feel the energy!' I could tell he *was* the Master and this was no place to come for a bit of R&R. Mimicking the others, I tentatively proceeded to shake on the spot as he held my wrist in a firm but gentle manner for about five minutes. I maintained my gaze upon the large photo of the Master, Ratu, perched on the front wall of the taman. What seemed like an hour passed, as my mind began to seek an escape from the mundane act I was pushing my body through.

The people shaking around me seemed to be building in intensity, their pounding movements becoming faster and more purposeful. Sweat was pouring from all of us and squeals of pain filled the air louder and more aggressively. Suddenly, my mind silenced and I found myself entering into a shaking rhythm where I could not and did not want to stop. I began to feel aches from various parts of my body, as something inside had been triggered and just did not want to stop. 'Electric! Electric!' Ratu ordered to us all, as the screams from some scared me back into thought: *What type of place is this?* Ratu walked among us, placing his hand on our backs and wrists and working us up with his mantra: 'Electric! Electric!' People suddenly began shouting out as loud as can be, and then falling onto the floor in a climactic finale, pulsating and panting in a puddle of sweat. I did not want to stop. My skin began to itch all over as though hundreds of tiny irritants were tearing their way out from beneath my skin. I continued pounding my weight hard into the floor to the point where I felt like I was floating on air, riding a mystical horse through the sky.

Eventually, after what seemed like hours of non-stop shaking, my body crumbled beneath me and I fell to the ground. With my eyes closed and my heartbeat drumming feverishly, I felt pure joy, inner contentment and peace. I lay there on the floor completely numbed-out, unable to even lift my arm for what seemed like an eternity. In the unfamiliar stillness of my mind a strange empty void grew larger and larger. When I found the strength and clarity to sit myself up, I saw that Ratu had left the taman and the others were sitting and bowing, their faces obviously looking worked over. 'Wow, what was that?' I sighed. Introductions followed and my curiosity was eagerly looking for answers to what I had just experienced. 'That was energy, bro,' replied one guy, his eyes like two full moons piercing the night sky.

Exiting the taman, I felt like I had just finished some crazy ride at an amusement park, with that look of pleasurable disbelief. Ketut was there waiting for me with a huge smile on her face. She asked me how the shaking was. 'I'm not sure... very powerful,' I said. I had instantly grown to love her smile and angelic presence. There seemed to be about six or so rooms adjoining a small house, which I guessed was Ratu's residence. Ketut showed me to my room, being the standard Balinese budget type — basic and 'it'll do'. There were two single beds, a couple of side tables and a rope strung across the back wall with a few coat hangers on it. Hot water was one luxury I would have to do without in this part of the island.

I was sharing a room with a hard-looking guy who had introduced himself in the taman as James, from England. Although he seemed quite friendly and articulate, I wasn't ready to ask too many questions. Due to my anxiety, I was fearful of sharing a room with someone. I was coming down in a new and unfamiliar environment and wasn't sure what type of weird space I would end up at.

After a cold, yet refreshing, shower I attended dinner and was introduced to the others. Even though everyone was friendly, it was difficult. We all sat in close proximity to each other and I felt emotionally on-edge. Whatever it was I felt in the taman had subsided. The food was delicious. 'Made with 100% love!' said James. A couple of people were saying nothing and left immediately after their meal was finished, maybe feeling anxious like myself or exhausted. I was both. I dropped a few questions about what I had experienced in the taman, but everyone seemed reluctant to burden my mind with explanations.

'This journey is beyond the limitations of our minds,' said the middle-aged man with a French accent, who introduced himself as Eric. 'We learn to feel here and in feeling we connect to ourselves and life, and that is where you receive all the information you need. Life's true meaning will share itself with you when you become more sensitive. Keep going, Paul, it's there waiting for you to find. Shake with focus and purpose and that's how you will receive it.'

'How shall I focus?'

'When you are shaking, try and keep your mind free from any thoughts that you can wander off with. And it's important to keep saying the mantra, *Om Swastiastu*, which means may God shower grace upon you.'

After dinner I attended meditation in the taman with Ratu, the Balinese and Westerners. My mind was on a continual loop, racing from one thought to the other. Afterwards, everyone stayed and continued sitting. One of the traits I admire in the Balinese is their ease at sitting and being, with no need to continually force conversation. I found it challenging. I was used to clubbers or myself anxiously raving on and on, avoiding silence. Everyone was seemingly comfortable and peaceful sitting in silence. Ratu then began chatting and laughing with his Balinese friends in the front of the taman, yet there was no address forthcoming to me or the Westerners.

The Balinese women left the taman and then one of the Balinese men rolled some type of cigarette. I moved next to an old man who introduced himself as Putu. I asked what it was. 'Tobacco,' he said. I immediately thought, *Tobacco, of all things!*

This place keeps getting more bizarre. The old Balinese man told me in very broken English that this tobacco was blessed and sacred, and very different from what we purchase in the supermarket, as the packaged tobacco was used for the purpose of the lower *astral* and had lost its sacred spirit. 'Sacred tobacco is medicine!' he said, as he joined his hands in prayer pose and gave thanks as it was being passed to him. I thought, *Whatever*, as he passed it on to me. It felt like a huge session, with each man drawing and passing it along. When I drew on the reefer-like paper, and the smoke entered my lungs, it almost tore them apart. It was more excruciating than the cheapest hash I had ever had and I coughed for almost half an hour, as Ratu and the others laughed. Then, exhausted, I went to bed and it was the most peaceful night's sleep I could remember.

The following morning my roommate woke me at 6 a.m. and I lethargically entered another intense shaking session in the taman. Ratu was there, working us all into a frenzy. Again, I felt some type of euphoria battling with my anxiety and my back was aching. After two-and-a-half hours I couldn't give anymore and I bemoaned exactly that to Ratu. He said to me, 'You focus and ask to take energy!' I pushed on for another half an hour and then the session finished. I was exhausted, but feeling energised, optimistic and somewhat grounded, with a fire in my eyes not experienced for quite some time.

At breakfast, I asked James how often we shake: 'Three-hour sessions, three times every day!' This place seemed to be some type of off-the-beaten-track boot camp, not the easygoing spiritual haven I was expecting. It reminded me of one of those survivor shows, with a mix of different personalities and attitudes all thrown together. I could sense friendliness from most of the other Westerners, even though I only really felt ease of conversation so far with James and Eric. Some others simply kept to themselves. I didn't know if I had the patience to continually push my mind and body for three sessions a day, but this pain was not like what I had been living with for so long now. Even with this mixed assembly of Westerners, the warmth and kindness of the Balinese besotted me. I felt like I was at home — really at home.

That night, before the shaking session began, I went to Ratu to explain my overall situation. Before I had the chance to convey my words, he just lit up again with a whopping smile and said, 'No problem, energy can fix. Just you shake!' Ratu seemed somewhat distant from me, almost arrogant towards me. I wanted pity and acknowledgment from him, but it was not to be, which stirred anger within me. I shook with an incredible amount of anger, frustrated at what seemed like a disregard for me. The session was again full-on bedlam — the most intense exertion I felt I had ever engaged in. Again, I shook myself through the anger, the physical pain and thoughts to stop all of this nonsense. Then I hit that space again where I felt some force was carrying me and I could not stop. It was like the shaking was moving me into another state.

Exhausted after a full day's training and with my muscles fatigued, I fell to my bed to the soothing sound of the Balinese chanting their Hindu prayers. Soon after, both my ears suddenly blocked, much like the feeling of rising in an aircraft, though I couldn't 'pop' them open. The pressure kept on building to the point where it seemed like a balloon full of razors was inflating and forcing its way through my ears. I had never felt pain like it. James kept telling me to trust the *process*. I eventually compelled myself into the taman, where Ratu was seated chatting to his Balinese friends. Feeling scared and concerned, and with tears almost weeping down my face, I tried to explain my predicament to him and, to my astonishment, he let out a huge laugh and flippantly said, 'Good process, you no worry.' He then turned his attention back to his friends. Bewildered and in agony, I about-faced to literally crawl back to my room when Ratu laconically said, 'You play music, ya?' I turned to him with a blank, 'Yes.' He smiled warmly, again with his repeat of, 'Good process. You no worry.'

Lying back on my bed, the pain kept building and intensifying to the point where I was ready to call a doctor, a crazy notion, given my location. Suddenly and dramatically, one ear popped with a lacerative tear, relieving the pain in an instant. About five minutes later the other ear followed. The abrupt subsidence eased my worried mind, but when a trickle of liquid began to ooze from both ears, I wondered, *What is going on here?* Eventually I fell asleep, relieved in one way, but bewildered in another.

The following morning I felt sick with some type of fever, unable to find the strength to get out of bed. My ears were still leaking something unpleasant. I was only spending a few days there and time was precious, and being sick wasn't on my agenda, though I kept wondering just what type of place I had really entered.

'This practice is a powerful journey, transcending different levels of oneself and you are now experiencing the standard introduction we call *process*,' said my roommate, with a huge, gaping smile. 'To heal and grow, you must cleanse the body of all the "dirt" you have accumulated. Your sickness is a great sign of cleaning and, should you decide to continue on, more processes could push you to your very limits. Beyond those boundaries you will find what you have been seeking. Your ears and fever are process,' he said, 'your healing has begun. Wherever you need healing, the energy works deeply and very powerfully on your body, mind, emotions and spirit. Ratu has given us a way to heal ourselves by ourselves. Once our sacred fire energy is woken up by the shaking, it hits blocks and produces illness to release them. These blocks have been created on an energetic level and are felt/expressed through the physical. The physical symptoms are manifestations of deeper illnesses.'

It was all a bit much, but I felt a connection to what he was telling me. I realised that my ear process was related to my DJ work, with the use of headphones and loud, heavy music pulsating continuously into my ears. I reflected on Ratu's comment the previous night, and wondered how he knew. I thought I may have mentioned it to Ketut, but I wasn't sure. Some profound force had miraculously honed in on some corner of my lifestyle and begun to work on another, deeper level of cleansing. Prior to this process, I had pain all over my body, except in my ears.

James rallied me to get myself into the taman, where I felt compelled to push myself through the pain of my fever and the discomfort of my leaking ears. Again, I began another shaking session and the battle raged inside my mind. Ratu was working us all up again and people were going mad, screaming, laughing and some were throwing up. Some of the Balinese were holding long krisses and wooden snakes, and seemed to be trancing out. It was very powerful and I couldn't help but take my focus off the shake and comprehend all that was happening around me. Ratu walked up to me and pulled a large piece of tobacco from his mouth. He tore it in two and stuffed the pieces into my ears. He then smiled at me and motivated me to shake stronger. I had not encountered a discipline like this before, but I felt like I had no options — like there was no tomorrow. Everyone was giving it their best and the Balinese were strong, supportive and devoted. It was awe-inspiring. The end of the session was welcomed and I couldn't believe I got through it.

Mealtime was again tense. I could sense a couple of the other people were tense — I certainly was. I wanted answers and sympathy. Nothing made any sense. One moment I was feeling the best I had felt in years and the next I was keeled over in pain I had never known existed in me. Everyone just smiled and said, 'Good process. Shake strong now.' A few of the other Westerners shared with me their stories of healing themselves from serious sickness via shaking.

Troy, a guy from Ireland said, 'I was an alcoholic and I found
out I had hepatitis and my organs were failing. Then I found the
shaking practice and began to understand energy, and slowly I
healed myself and got my life back on track. I should be dead
now. Once you understand the energy, all things are possible.'
Then Lara, a woman from Belgium, added, 'You have to trust that
the way you are feeling now is very positive. We must get our
negative manifestations out, and the only way we can do that is
through process. You are doing fine. Many weird processes
happen here,' she said, as she raised her trousers exposing
numerous large welts covering her legs. It looked incredible, like
volcanic pustules scattered across her skin. Her words of support
were heartfelt, but I was not only puzzled by what I was hearing
and feeling, but also by what I was seeing erupting from her legs.

Intense shaking, people sick, throwing up, screaming, crying,
laughing — nothing made any sense. I was getting a total work-
over, with my mind continually screaming at me to get out,
though just a thought about returning to Australia snapped me
back into this opportunity I had stumbled across. I had to push
on and see where it would take me. I could feel a huge battle
raging inside me to stop all of this and my almost childish
questioning was sensed by the others that I was vulnerable but
open and ready to travel into the unknown. The Westerners were
urging me to keep going. The ones I had been engaging had a
dogged determination, which I felt inspiring. Even though their
stories seemed rather tall about healing themselves of serious
sickness through simply shaking, their conviction was
unmoving. And the majority of them — apart from a couple of
people who seemed in a worse state than me — seemed normal
every-day people. They were certainly not the trashed dance
party crowd I had become accustomed to or some ragged hippies
on the love-conquers-all trip. They all seemed genuine. But I was
waiting for Ratu to give us some type of lesson or information;
yet it was not forthcoming. 'When you become more sensitive,

you will get all the information you need,' Eric said.

The following day, my fever had subsided, yet my ears were still leaking something. At the dinner table my curiosity was now eager for more information. I intuitively asked the others some questions. I could see by their faces that they were holding back. I must have looked like a new apprentice wanting to be a tradesman overnight. I shared my job and lifestyle with everyone and they couldn't believe the way the scene really was. I said that it had left quite a mess in its wake.

'Paul, when you focus during the shaking and give your best — one, your body will heal itself of whatever it is you have been struggling with and, two, you will discover the energy that has created those problems and kept you in the negative patterns. They go hand-in-hand,' said Eric, quite direct and serious.

'Energy? What energy could that be?' I naïvely replied.

'When you are ready to see it, it will be there. From what you just told us about your lifestyle, it's definitely there. If you are not ready or are attached to your old ways, it will remain hidden from you. But if your desire to heal is as strong as your curiosity, certain things will appear to guide you and show you what lies behind the veil.' Eric came across as very confident. He person- ified the gentleness of the French, with his soft, calming accent complementing his tall, slender frame. Yet I felt a strength emanating from him. He didn't look sick and I didn't know if he had any problems. I guessed he was some type of healer. He never mentioned it and I didn't ask.

'Has Ratu taught you this?' I continued, eager to fish for more information.

'Ratu motivates us to shake. It is you who wakes up. No one else can wake you up. If you shake with the right focus and intent, the answers appear. The answers are ever-present, available to everyone with introspection. Shaking is the way we become sensitive and is a means to obtain information. The energy and introspective message is in the shake — and it's not just any shake, as that would make shaking simply a sport. You must shake with focus and connect to the energy.'

'To what energy?'

'To the sacred universal fire within you — essential *bio-energy*. It's always been there; it is nature's source. It's in you *and* all around you.'

I then asked why Ratu hasn't really talked to me yet, my words laced with frustration.

'Because you want to speak and know from your mind,' Eric replied, with a calming pat on my shoulder. 'When you have nothing to say, then you can communicate with him,' he wittily humoured. 'You have to experience feeling to then understand, and when you understand through feeling, then you will talk from your heart, not your head. And you will always talk less from your heart than your head.'

'Well I certainly can't contest the fact that I'm totally locked in my mind. Now it makes sense. A wise man, talking to a gibbering party animal isn't really a clear channel for communication. But this practice seems so odd; I'm trying to understand it.'

'This practice is not so much a practice. When you work with sacred fire energy — or astral energy, or the vibrational field as it's also called — it cannot be explained by a theory or structure, nor rationalised with the mind. Everything is energy. No doubt being a DJ you would have felt the power of working with energy and the crowd. Even though it was a negative energy, it was still energy at play. You couldn't theorise working a crowd with drugs and energy, could you? Or could you practice it? You'd already know to a degree that energy is communicative and influential through your job. Well if — or I should say, when — you become more sensitive, you will truly understand the language of energy, and then you'll be able to discern all that is encompassed within it. That's when you'll know and ultimately understand exactly what you have been working with — and living with — for all these years. We are working with nature's source and nature doesn't explain its ways, but in realigning ourselves with nature we become aware and then we understand.'

Eric then excused himself from the table and I sat for a moment thinking about DJing and the way I used to take the crowd on a journey throughout the night with the music, feeling the mood and the seduction, and then working with it. I also thought about the drugs and how they captivated an amazing feeling of energy within the crowd and me. We all entered into another level of reality. *Yeah, energy!* I thought to myself, *I've been working with it all along. But how did it all bring me so unstuck?*

After another evening meditation, in which I slowly found some respite from the barrage of thoughts, I lay in my bed reflecting on what I had been told at the dinner table earlier. James entered the room and we began chatting. It wasn't long before I found myself complaining about my state and how I was always anxious in the proximity of others. James smiled and said, 'Paul, no doubt you are suffering at the moment, but no matter which way you continue on in life, pain will be there. But you have a choice. Your life was in decline right up to the moment you walked through these gates and if you never found a way to understand energy and free yourself, your pain would have taken your life eventually, with a lot worse pain than you have experienced up to now. Now the other pain is process. If you can accept the fact that freeing yourself means processing the negative living within you, to really burn the core of your suffering, then, over time, as you clean out all the crap inside, your pain will clear and you can go on to live a healthy life — and die with a smile on your face, an old man. Process means a type of clearing pain, but, without process, pain is soul destructive.'

James looked like the type of guy who wouldn't mince his words and I wasn't surprised at his direct advice. He seemed a bit of a joker, but there was no nonsense. There was no room for half-hearted efforts or flimsy attitudes. I thought spiritual people were supposed to be soft and weak, but he and most of the others personified the guy-next-door types. I found it easy with James because he didn't portray himself as too dignified or saintly. That realness helped me fit in because I was far from a dignified or saintly type of guy myself.

'I'm not sure if I can sustain this level of commitment. Okay, if I'm here for a few days I can push with you all and I feel an incredible amount of power and support, but back home it's just me and my old life. I'm scared of falling into the same old ways,' I uttered, unable to mask the lost little boy I felt I was.

He looked at me, holding a moment's silence, and said, 'Paul, many people around the world are waking up to the state of the planet and humanity. You sitting here talking to me now is not by chance. People are ready — you are ready. What we want to understand is the source of ourselves, beyond theories or religious dogma. We are shaking here to raise our level of vibration and awareness. But no matter what you do, even if it's yoga, if you are working with a vibrational activity and are not aware of the *true* dynamics of astral energy, then you can shake all you like, stretch yourself like a rubber band, and you will not be able to receive the right information or obtain true awareness. You may obtain body awareness, but not deeper, greater, higher astral awareness. Actually, you can accelerate the negative.'

Looking back at James, my attentive silence was more about my mind trying to absorb all he was telling me. But I was interested. Very interested. He continued, 'It's not so much about the shaking practice per se, it's about opening up to and feeling the energy — which is information — and becoming aware of what is manifesting around you, and from within you. I'm on a journey of understanding through feeling and this is where I can connect with people of like-minds to share and support and encourage. The world is filling up with the likes of myself and others here. We are out there. If you open up to the energy, the entire world is a teacher — every corner of it.

'When you go back home, Paul, don't worry about intensity; just commit yourself to finding the sacred fire within you. Open yourself to the world around you by working to see what you haven't been able to before. Trust me, brother, the information you are looking for is there in front of you. It's always been there every moment of every day of your life. Look for it and, when you finally see it, you will realise things are different from what they appear. And when you begin to really see through feeling, life becomes clear. Then you can make the right choices and you will understand what living really is. Your old ways will no longer resonate with you, slowly but surely, if you want to open up to what is available to you.'

Like a child hearing a fascinating bedtime story, I said exactly that to James. 'This sounds like a fascinating bedtime story. What you are telling me feels as though I've been waiting to know this — really know it from within — all my life. But I'm still scared about my past. I pushed it pretty hard and I'm worried I've done irreparable damage.'

'Paul, the more you shake and process, the more you can understand energy — not from what I or others tell you, but through feeling it yourself. You *can* shed the past and harmonise with the positive universal vibration. Healing is just the beginning. Healing is available to everyone who understands the dynamics of energetic vibrations. Beyond that, the right experiences and people — and tests — will appear to help you choose the right way to really live life. Like I said, you are not here by chance. You created the connection to experience all of this. You needed to connect with people who could show you the initial way. But only you can walk it, and you will only see your personal path if you want to open your heart to it. We all have to do the hard yards on our own.'

I suddenly realised how I had ended up there. I had been looking for a holistic practitioner in Sydney and out of dozens of names in the phone book I randomly chose one. It was that uncanny magnetism of synchronicity, which aligned me with the right practitioner offering me the information about Ratu. If I had not gone to that practitioner, or had chosen another one, I would not have stumbled upon this opportunity.

Again I thought of DJing and working with drugs, music and the crowd. Trying to see it from an energetic perspective, I could visualise how I was tapping into a universal force of negative energy, which would ultimately bring me down. Things were beginning to seem less bizarre and more plausible. I recalled a book I had read by Lynne McTaggart, *The Field,* where science was beginning to uncover the universal power of energy. What I was now hearing from the others — about energy being intelligent — reminded me of her research. It was like this other world I had experienced for so long was actually universal science, although academics were only touching the surface. Here I was, with a group of people, working with this scientific frontier I had read about as being just out of reach of proven science. Relative to my experiences on drugs though, it was still a mystery to me. I thanked James and drifted off to a sleep of new possibilities.

After the next morning's shake and breakfast, I wanted to engage the Balinese more. I went to the kitchen where the women were preparing food and offerings. They were all laughing and their joy was filling the room. 'Food made with 100% love,' I remembered James saying. The kitchen was a far cry from any Western standard. Being in a remote part of a Third World country, squeaky-clean bench tops and floors weren't a priority. The pungent smell of coconut oil lingered in the air, which had been the main cooking oil in Bali well before Western influence. I always believed that the smell of coconut oil would make a powerful crowd disperser. But that tribal authenticity added to the entire experience — raw and real. Tropical fruits and vegetables were stacked against the walls, and the women were seated on the floor peeling onions and garlic with home-made knives. I sat down on the floor next to the women, feeling very much a part of a tribal clan.

The women were curious about me. Being Western, I found that always drew interest from the Balinese. When I told them I worked at the local nightclub, they all jokingly shuddered. '*Narkoba!*' they giggled.

'Yes, drugs,' I replied. I shared with them that drugs were the reason I was there, and I was trying to discover the truth behind drugs and my sickness.

One of the women, Wayan, who looked fit and strong, spoke better English than the others. She had spent time in the West and her English *was* good — better than most Balinese. She portrayed a Western-type of confidence, although maintaining a peaceful demeanour. She responded somewhat hesitantly, 'Drugs are the dark spirits of the astral.'

I had read about the astral, but reading about it sort of kept it 'out there', like it was simply a literary concept or as tangible as Moses parting the Red Sea. But there in the ashram it was referred to often, like it was here, now, and my reason for being there.

'What exactly is the astral, Wayan?'

'The astral is the spirit world. There are different levels and how you live your life determines what level of the astral influences it. The Balinese Hindu's aim is to live by the highest level and when they die their soul will transcend. This island is not called the Island of the Gods for nothing. The astral world is a continual battle between good and bad, and we humans are a part of that battle. You must stay focused.'

'But how does the astral work with drugs?'

'Drugs are *Maya*.'

'Maya! What is Maya?' my naïvety still portraying the novice.

'Maya means illusion — or delusion. Many people believe that drugs are the truth of their experience — that what they are entering is real. If it is real, why do drugs end in suffering and destroy lives? *The Vedas*, which are the Hindu scriptures, speak of

Maya as the pathway to hell. Drugs are probably one of the most powerful expressions of Maya. They lift you to what you believe to be an incredible place quickly, but instead take you to the domain of the lower astral dimension. And the lower dimension is the gateway to hell.'

'But it doesn't make sense. My initial feelings were love and bliss and connectedness, but, yes, they ended up quite dark and scary.'

'Yes, drugs are the devil wrapped in the delusion of Maya. Maya is our test in this life. Maya can be drugs, cigarettes, power, greed, unloving sex, shopping — and for many all of those. Those desires can offer you the mind illusion of feeling good, but none lead to the path of truth. Look at tobacco. It is a sacred plant, but we know what it does to people who don't respect its spiritual powers and use it for the purpose of Maya. We are here in this life to break free of these temptations which can suffocate our souls. Beware of your desires. To break free is to really win in this life. To fail means to become a slave to your weaknesses — to the delusion of Maya and to the servitude of the lower astral.

'Can you tell me, Paul, why do drugs end in suffering?'

'No, I can't. I believe that they simply mess up your body due to too much toxicity.'

'Yes, they do mess up your body, but before your body fails, your astral body changes. The state of your physical body is a consequence of your energetic state, which is a direct influence of the astral dimensions. You make many choices every day as to which level of the astral world you choose to align with. From the subtlest of thoughts, to the desire of drugs, to the people and places you choose to be near, heaven and hell is your free choice every day. Failure of your body took place well before you became toxic and realised you were sick, and it took place in the astral world, of which you and every human is connected to. The reason the world is in such a mess is because humanity is consciously and unconsciously aligning with the lower astral dimensions. Humanity is blinded by the illusion of Maya through the ego and the mind.'

I sat listening to Wayan with my eyes starry and amazed. It was a revelation, but it all made complete sense. I continued. 'This would then explain why I was seeing demons when going to sleep and in my dreams, and why my mind was a mess to the point of being on the verge of suicidal.'

'Of course, but the majority of people refuse to accept that the spirit world could be the cause of their ills. They believe drugs are a way for them to experience a hidden part of themselves. It is Maya, Paul. The delusion has them believe that they are on the path of truth, but they are not. And what do they want to do? Like most drug users who experience the power of drugs, they do it again and again, which becomes an embodiment of the lower astral world. Their souls are not free. It is their minds that become full with what they believe is truth, but the state of their energetic body becomes sick. The dark forces of the astral world steal your life force.'

'Now it makes sense to me why many clubs are filled with gothic and even demonic decor. It's complementary to everyone's journey with drugs.'

'When Hindus prepare a ceremony, we place different offerings to the Gods to align ourselves to the highest realms of the astral. When clubs and parties prepare their venues, well, you know of the offerings and the thoughts and actions of all those who attend.' With a smile that lit up the room, and her focus returning to the food preparation as if to say enough for now, Wayan, with an abeyant look concluded, 'Beware of the energy of Maya, Paul.'

I thanked Wayan and the other women and went outside and sat in the courtyard, watching the children playing and taking in all that had been shared. My thoughts moved from the conversation I had just had, as I was captivated by the people before me. *So much harmony,* I thought to myself. I reflected on Bali and village life. I continued to be humbled by how different it is from the West — men in sarongs, who were soft and sweetly spoken, yet strong, and women — beautiful, graceful and every superlative of the sacred feminine. Family values, a rich and loving attitude to the spiritual, were upheld by every village and its people, and spread from the waters washing to the shores to the lunar-like stones that sit atop the mountain peaks. Dedication to a spiritual life manifested itself everywhere — from the ornate ceremonies through to the protective blessing of a motorbike. Offerings to the astral world were a commitment undertaken by the entire island.

I saw old-man Putu seated nearby and I went over and sat next to him. He and most of the other Balinese lived in the ashram. It was hard to tell which couples were together and which children belonged to who, as everyone typified a communal life, where everyone was taking care of all the children — even the older children took care of the younger ones with maturity. Putu placed his arm around my shoulder and kept it there. This is a sign of friendship in Bali. I still felt quite uncomfortable having people too close to me so I pulled away. My discomfort didn't seem to register with him or he didn't seem to care about it. I asked him how long he had been shaking.

'Long time,' he said. 'Shaking very powerful. Must stay focused.' Etched with wrinkles that all seemed to run upwards, Putu smiled like that expression fitted snugly into each grafted line, and had done so all his long life. Looking at me with his glassy eyes, weathered but sparkling like crystal, he then held my hand. His hand felt like sandpaper and although he was very lean and small, just the hold of his hand felt as though he was as strong as an ox. He continued, 'You no stop shaking. Important keep going.'

Mimicking his simple English, I replied, 'Back home, maybe difficult, Putu. Many party. Many narcoba. Me, many problem.'

He laughed, and I think I only saw two teeth, which made me

smile, more about him not caring about the way he looked than anything derogatory towards him. He pulled me closer, still holding my hand with a wrench-like grip. 'Energy will cut past life. Important you trust energy. Past will finish. Energy always know best, give you best. Energy very clever.' He then looked over my shoulder, and stood up saying, 'Ya, ya, good,' and simply walked off. I loved the simple way that these people acted. There was no political correctness. It was silence, or say what has to be said and that's it — finished.

After what would be my final evening session, Ratu instructed us all to remain in the taman. *Finally,* I thought, *an address from Ratu.* Ratu's greeting of 'Om Swastiastu' was reciprocated by us all, followed by silence. He held the tender silence of the room for quite some time, his eyes scanning all of us and then looking above our heads, as if he were tuning into our thoughts.

With Wayan translating, Ratu began by saying, 'Working with the energy, with shaking, is pure spirituality. We can feel the showering of the soul inside. Our spiritual connection is with our soul, not our mind. God cannot be grasped with the mind. Here, we focus on how we can connect our soul with our body and quieten our mind. Here, in order to think less, we shake more. If shaking is difficult, it's because we have two energies inside fighting — our mind wants to stop and our heart wants to train. Our mind always looks for problems and makes life difficult. Why is life short? Because it is eaten by the mind. If the soul is the driver, people will live a long life. The soul always searches for a way that our body can live long and happy, because our soul always wants the best for us. With our soul alive, it will look for what there is in our body. If there is something lacking in our body — for example, an organ is not functioning — the soul will neutralise it with bio-energy.

'Every cell in your body knows your soul and works together as one. But when your mind thinks you are something other than your soul, you are not one with your body. Then you get sick.

You must acknowledge you are your soul, not your mind, and become one. Humans are like cells in the body. If everyone becomes one with their soul, then humanity becomes one with each other. But if humanity follows the mind and the ego, then we are not one. Humanity turns on itself like sick cells turn on the body. But it is not the mind that is the problem — it's the dark energy, and the frequency, that keeps the mind in a prison. If you follow your mind, how can you liberate your mind? That's why you must follow your heart.'

Ratu again held the silence of the room for quite some time, looking at us all and above our heads. He then continued, 'Now in the world it is very easy to get what you want because there is a lot of darkness in the world. It's easy to get what the mind wants. To get what the soul wants is more difficult. There are many tests. Life is about tests. It's important not to connect to the mind.'

Ratu then called one of the Balinese men up to the front and instructed something in Balinese. The man then placed his hands in prayer position and began shaking, building in intensity. Continuing to shake strong, he then screamed out loud and fell to the floor at Ratu's feet and began laughing. Ratu stood there and scanned the room, looking at us all directly. He then said in English himself, 'The Balinese here with Ratu, shaking for seventeen years. Their life about offering to the divine. Shaking with proper focus, connect you to divine. You have problem, you shake, you focus on divine energy. The Balinese shaking and offering, connect Ratu to the West. The more people shake and connect to divine, more big, grow the focus on one. Many people with strong focus, bigger than Himalaya. Then problem in the world lose strength. Important every person take responsibility. People who understand energy, very lucky. Important to shake with good focus, then problem no more.'

Ratu then thanked us all and left the taman. His talk inspired me. Simply listening to this wise man instilled a sense of worthiness inside me. I felt humbled to be sitting there listening to him. I could have sat there for hours, but from what I was beginning to understand, less is more. Deeper understanding would come by raising my vibration and connecting to the divine source of the universe — the higher astral. And to do that, shaking with the proper focus was the way. What was taking place within me felt truly like a beautiful transformation; but processing was showing me the reality of my life in that moment. It was a tug-of-war, showing me, not only where I was at, but also where I could go.

Before his talk, Ratu seemed a bit of a mystery. He was always around the ashram, praying, doing offerings and talking to the Balinese, but I felt like an outsider because he didn't really give me any attention — more so, he never gave my mind any attention. But after listening to his talk, even though it was simple, I felt I was in the right place, with the right help. I could feel he cared about us and wanted us to discover ourselves. We had all the tools available to us every moment of every day. It was our responsibility as individuals to respect our lives and understand the way to really live.

That evening after dinner, Eric passed by my room where James and I had just began chatting. 'How has your first step towards the real you been, Paul?' said Eric, smiling as he entered the room.

'I feel like I've been run over by a truck and then nursed by a dozen princesses.'

'The initial journey is like that. Process, progress, process, progress, but slowly the processes ease and change.'

James said, 'When I first began shaking, I was laid up quite a few times with all sorts of physical releases. Now, I've cleared the physical energetic blocks, I'm processing subtle inharmonious mind traits which I can now see and which are deeper layers of my negative state and the seeds of my sickness. I need to stay on top of life and ultimately move into my heart — that's where the journey goes for me. That's where it goes for all of us. To get there, I need to continually work with the energy. Not quite *living* from the heart yet, but I'm healthy now, loving life and working *with* the energy is certainly softening the ticker.'

I felt comfortable now to ask James and Eric what their problems were before they started working with energy.

'I've never had any serious sickness,' said Eric, 'but through shaking and understanding the astral, I began to see how I was living in denial. I always held this ideal that I was a spiritual person — vegetarian, prayerful and perfect in my eyes. But as time passed and I processed more, I could see that my ideal was a trick of my ego, and I placed myself above others. Over time I realised that my subtle attitude was separating me from other people. I've worked to discard my ego's negative power. I've had to loosen up, as they say.'

James then shared, 'I was diagnosed with a sickness some years ago, and, even with conventional medicine, my chances of a long life were short. I heard about the shaking practice and went to a session in London. I embraced shaking as a way of life and, well, the rest is history — no medicine, no more sickness. It was more than simply turning up to a shaking session each week. I had to honour the astral world and, with introspection, find the negativity that was cutting my life short. Once you work with the energy, if you really want to discover your own truth, problems — no matter how large or small — can be overcome. As you become sensitive to the sacred fire energy within you, information appears to allow you to make a choice whether to use or play with that energy, or detach and discard it. But to see and continue living your negative traits would inhibit your growth and healing — and actually have grave karmic consequences.'

'But I still don't fully understand the relationship between processing and this energetic information you are telling me about,' I said.

James looked at me with that tough but sweet look I now felt comfortable with. 'The shaking practice is a means to raise our vibration. The world is in a bit of a mess at the moment because too many are resonating at a low frequency and doing all sorts of crazy stuff and falling like raindrops. As a consequence of not resonating harmoniously with the love of the universe, turmoil and sickness is the manifestation.'

Eric interrupted, 'My father is a surgeon in France, but some of his colleagues have cancer. The doctor you go to for help with cancer has it himself. What people don't realise is that when they go to a doctor and get, say, a tumour removed, the surgery cannot address the vibrational alignment to the lower astral that manifested that tumour. You leave a bit lighter, physically, but energetically you haven't changed a thing. If one truly wishes to clear the entirety of their sickness — the tumour *and* the lower astral vibrational alignment — it has to be energetically burned by moving into a higher frequency.

'Negativity is becoming all-consuming. Doctors, patients — no one is spared. Humanity's vibration needs to rise and processing is the reality we must face to break free of the lower astral. We, here, process via shaking. Remember, shaking awakens you to another level, but to be truly free of the negative, lower astral, you must become aware of your dark and inharmonious mind traits that hold you in a low vibration pattern. And when you see your own, you will see how the world really does spin.'

'But shaking cannot be the only way to raise one's vibration?' I suggested.

James, with a slight chuckle, which I felt was due to my insatiable palate for more, added, 'The ancient arts, such as yoga or tai chi, are vibrational practices, yet most of these ancient traditions have become tainted with manifestations of the astral's lower vibrational field. Many teachers in the West are teaching from their own dark energies. It's not the practice; it's the facilitator. Maybe through ego, greed, arrogance or sexual conquests or simply not resonating strongly — whatever state they are in, they instill those energies onto their students. Students may be able to master their poses, but if they are not aware of the myriad subtle negative energetic actions, true growth is beyond their reach.'

'Wow, my yoga teacher did a nine-week yoga teacher's course, and I found out he was a party guy, taking ecstasy and sleeping with some of his students,' I said.

'That's pretty extreme,' replied James. 'There wouldn't be many practitioners like that, but it's those energies that he carries and follows that inhibit all those whom he teaches. Plus, nine weeks seems a bit quick in understanding and then teaching an ancient vibrational science.'

Eric, with an affirmative nod said, 'It's not a coincidence that you aligned *yourself* with a person such as your yoga teacher who shared your energetic pattern — sex and drugs. What you resonate, will find an energetic complementary. Even complementary opposites are part of the lower astral's battle for dominance, such as victim/victimiser, seduced/seducer, poor/wealthy, healthy/suffering and needed/needy. Paul, this is what we've been telling you. The astral energetic world is a force of intelligence and a game of light versus dark, where the lower resonance of the populous now is aligning man with the intelligence of that negative realm, intent to rob humanity of its life force. When you leave and return home tomorrow, begin to open your heart and eyes to all that is in front of you. Look and feel what energy is playing. Look around you; its dynamics are everywhere.'

'How have you guys learnt all of this?'

'Paul, you could read a thousand books, see a hundred healers, but, if you don't want to *feel*, then all you are doing is filling your mind with clutter. And sometimes too much spiritual clutter can lead to the spiritual ego. You believe with your mind that you know the way to live free, when all you know is not what you exude energetically. Feeling is knowledge, not how many courses you have done, or what you know in your mind. People are so busy feeling gratuitous pleasures, or feeling the ego, they don't want to feel the truth. Read about it, tell about it, teach about it, write about it, yes, but to *feel* it is another matter. It's another state all together. People can talk and lecture all they want, but it is their body language — the state of it and how they act with it — that really tells the truth about what they exude energetically.

'Ratu gets us to shake with focus and then the rest is up to us. He can't instill truth; you have to feel it yourself. And when you feel it, then it resonates within you. That's why Ratu doesn't speak often to us. He has a method of raising our vibration and clearing our blocks — shake with focus. You can do it here in Bali or, like many now do around the world, within a group or in your bedroom at home. He is not here to inform; he's here to get us to feel. He's not a preacher; he's just a simple man with a way to raise our vibration. Shaking is tapping us into a space that is as old as the universe. And when you enter into it, you are learning the lessons of the universe. You become your own teacher/student.'

I began to acknowledge why reading so many books of discovery and self-help never really assisted my healing. I was simply filling my mind with information believing that understanding certain wisdoms or methods would help me. But I was not processing the lower astral alignment I had been living. I pondered my attachment to the gay scene. I said to the guys, 'I always wondered why I felt drawn to the underground gay scene. I wasn't interested in gay men, but I always felt some type of belonging to that type of loose and debauched crowd. It was as though I was a part of the freest, most expressive part of society.'

'What was drawn to that crowd,' said James, 'and certainly the whole dance party scene in general, was the spirit of the energy manifesting through you and all the others sharing that same journey of drugs and partying. Look at it. The entire scene is a cocktail of selfish experiences all wrapped up in a highly sensual and stimulating environment, which becomes an addictive comfort zone because there appears to be harmony. But that harmony is actually a lot of people all trying to grab hold of — in a selfish way — whatever they want in that moment without considering the consequences. That false harmony is the energy of drugs — your attraction to that scene. Those environments are nothing more than playing fields of the lower astral.'

I then said, 'Just as Wayan explained to me regarding Maya, it makes sense. But ecstasy and the entire scene seemed to be a connection to the heavens. It felt so real. If ever I was *feeling,* it was while peaking on ecstasy. There was a time, a moment, where I was connected to the heavens. Connected to my heart. I was sure of it.' They looked at each other and smiled. I felt a bit of an idiot. Deep down I knew drugs were some illusion because they totally wiped me out to the point I was an on-edge mess. Still smiling, but trying to regain a look of assistance, Eric seemed to feel more prepared to answer me. 'Drugs are nothing more than an alignment to the vibration of the lower astral, whether it's pot, cocaine, ecstasy, or some sedative/stimulant the doctor prescribes you. Drugs hold information that communicates with your body when taken. Ecstasy, for example, promotes a biological interchange — *and also* an energetic interchange. It's the energy that is the primary and superior reaction. What you are consuming is the spirit of the drug. Shamen from around the world have known of this energetic cocktail for millennia. They consume psychoactive plants to induce altered states of consciousness, and travel to the astral. I've met many on my spiritual path who are staunch believers of these plants, and they are certain that it's a gateway to heaven and wisdom. But they are naïve in believing that true spirituality — the liberation of the soul — can be achieved in consuming those plants.'

I interrupted with, 'But I can't help feeling convinced that ecstasy opens the heart and is some biblical catharsis, all-loving and divine.'

Eric continued, 'Ecstasy closes the heart. It's all a part of the astral world. The lower astral works its way through the mind and... I know this may sound hard to fathom, but drugs mask what is the ultimate truth — the truth of the soul. Drugs offer a mind illusion of the real thing in a fleeting experience, which the user is convinced is a divine shift in their consciousness. That moment of false enlightenment is a mental concept, induced by a vehicle of the lower astral — drugs. It's all information fed through the mind. One's vibration doesn't increase — drugs lower your vibration. The soul cannot transcend with drugs. It is very clever. Convince your mind and you become an advocate of that plane of galactic information, or that plane of love and bliss, never questioning that the plane you are floating across *is* in another dimension, but the wrong end of it.

'That puts the user in a very vulnerable and dangerous place. They return thinking that they are a bit wiser or a bit more loving, but the *reality* is they travelled to the lower astral world and they come back full of nasty hitchhikers. It all depends on what level of the astral you want to enter. When these drug-induced vibrational/astral voyages become abused, they are nothing more than a calling of dark universal energies, which over time builds a stronger channel/connection. You may start out on a blissful journey, but all of that bliss *is* the illusion — Maya — enticing you for more. Drugs are manipulators of the mind.

'Eventually, drugs are no longer needed to connect to the darker realms of the lower astral. The energetic information of that plane becomes a part of the person, manifesting itself through the mind, sickness in the body, and leaving you a spiritual energetic mess. You resonate at a lower frequency and, when that happens, all hell breaks loose. Drugs are a game of the super intelligent vibrational energies that fill our universe, but because we can't see them or science hasn't proven them, it's all rubbish in the eyes of the mainstream. And because drug users experience something so unbelievable, that experience is deemed absolute Divine Truth.'

'It's far from rubbish,' I said. 'I've experienced the power of Maya, and the aftermaths. I'm living proof of the game being played in perfect harmony — that is, if pain and despair is the harmony you seek. It was so powerful though. It was the only time in my life that I felt the power of my heart and connected to everyone and everything.'

James responded, 'Paul, if you felt love, why did it then make you feel disconnected and fall apart? Say you go to the doctor for something to treat your depression. You take a tablet and suddenly you are buzzing; well, you think you are buzzing. That too is an illusion of the mind. While the tablet biologically communicates with your body, and you believe you feel fine, the reality is you are channelling a connection to the lower astral through your commitment of "take one tablet in the morning and one at night". The tablets are a ticket to the lower astral plane. Why do you think drugs are now entrenched in history as destructive? And how many times do you hear about anti-depressants having horrendous — even suicidal — side effects? It's because of their energetic resonance.'

There was a moment's silence as the guys let me take in all they had been sharing. I always believed that there is no such thing as a miracle, or mystery. My view had been that everything has a scientific explanation. Last year's mystery is this year's scientific breakthrough. Humans have always been ever ready to disregard the unknown to the realms of fantasy. I knew my experiences on drugs were part of a scientific system, even though they were out of this world. But, hey, I couldn't grab hold of a radio signal, but that was flying invisibly through the air too, held information, and had come from a source. A hundred years ago, that was science fiction. In Bali, they lived for the astral world. I could finally see how I was living and playing with it for so long.

Eric continued, not with a tone of trying to convince me, but simply telling it as it was. 'Paul, universal lasting love is not a feeling you can call upon with some tiny tablet for a couple of hours, just as buzzing with life isn't instilled only while you are taking your medication, or have a head full of cocaine. It's your energetic body that is being filled with an illusion. Unfortunately, the real thing is something most people have swapped for the illusion. You've told us how drugs had you seeing all sorts of demons and thinking morbid depressive thoughts, even suicide. Like we keep telling you, the information is always right in front of us if we open ourselves up to discovering the truth. You certainly opened yourself up. You are living proof of living within the lower astral through drugs. There is an entire generation partying and taking drugs and connecting to the lower astral week-in, week-out.'

I began to feel quite overwhelmed, but what they were telling me felt right, and they were certainly saying it as it is. My experiences on drugs and the aftermaths were beyond anything any doctor or book could tell me. The amazing feelings seemed real, but the dark space that it led to also was just as real.

Eric looked at me with the eyes of truth, strong and direct, with a deep sense of peace. 'It's not only drugs. Sex, food, gambling — they all can give you a good feeling and a rush, but if not respected accordingly they all can tap you into a lower vibration through gluttonous seduction of the mind. Life is a dance upon a thin veil of light and dark, good or bad. It's how we focus our thoughts. That's why shaking with the proper focus is important. Look for it and seek to find it yourself. Every act, every day, ask yourself: "What energy am I resonating with this thought, this act or this reaction?" Then when you can discern the type of energy that is present, the choice is yours. If you can make the right choice — again and again — then you are truly living life.'

Trying to take it all in through the tobacco Ratu had been giving me daily to fill each of my still-leaking ears, James asked, as I poked the tobacco deeper into my ear canal, 'So how are your ears?'

'Still processing,' now well familiar with this new terminology.

'You're experiencing the power of the energy working through you. Isn't it amazing? You're working with it. You are ready.'

'I'll be glad when the leaking stops, but yeah, my time here training and meeting you guys *has* been amazing. It will be interesting when I go home. Something has definitely shifted. I'm ready to do whatever it takes to feel me again.'

'You're doing it bro; just keep on looking for the energy inside you and around you.'

'If I had never met you both I probably would have had a more challenging time here, trying to understand many things, so thanks.'

'Ratu works in a funny way. He wants us to feel the energy ourselves and then when we work with it and understand it, thus understanding ourselves and life, we can share our experiences with others. All of us here have different experiences with the astral energy's manifestation, but we are working with and understanding the same force. To many, even our old friends and family, all of this is bollocks, but then it's their journey. And, sadly, many of them are sick, but don't want to acknowledge that energy is the cause, and the cure.

'Much of what we've shared with you may not make sense right now, but if you can surrender to *trying* to work with the energy and you feel reactions and changes, then it is beginning to resonate within you, and then you are feeling but a speck of this force. Over time, the energy *will* change your life for the better and you will become a better person in every sense. You've already experienced and felt strongly the lower astral without knowing what was going on. Many people now, across the world, are questioning many things about the way our planet and lives are unfolding negatively and, at the root of it all, is energy at play — the wrong energy. If individuals begin to understand themselves from the perception of energy, power from the heart can move mountains.'

Now tired, I called it a day and wished my new friends a good night's sleep. As I lay my head onto the pillow, I reflected on the week that was and the craziness that awaited me when I returned home. The week had been a roller coaster of moments of pure bliss and intense, painful processes, erasing the thought that alternative healing was a passive journey. Surrounded by the beauty of Hinduism, this practice seemed to rise above all religious dogma. Each shaking session cut deep into painful blocks — physically, mentally and emotionally. That something missing feeling had finally found a channel in which to abate — naturally. I had found a place that on the surface made no sense but, surrendering, all the sense in the world. The comprehension of my past relationship within the chaos of my social scene and the inner peace I was trying to draw from ecstasy was finally obvious. It was a twisted engagement of Western revelling and artificial transcendence, splitting me to my very core. With shaking, I had found a channel in which to break free of the shackles of the past and reunite myself on every level.

Ratu's practice challenged me to *go back* into my pain to liberate myself from the seed of my suffering. There was no other way and it was a huge test. Drugs and the fast lane had made me sick and now shaking and processing required me to connect with and induce the innermost remnants of this misery. To burn the core and the entrenched memories of trauma with the sacred energetic fire, I would have to endure more discomfort layer by layer, literally stripping me down physically, mentally, emotionally and spiritually. Only then could I liberate myself in this life and truly live with purpose and evolve to be as I was meant to be.

I had discovered a precious gift through shaking. There was still a lot of work to do, an embrace of further challenges and a celestial mystery to unfold. Wanting to not sink into the abyss of social castoffs, finally my heart had found the right key to unlock its door. My heart had found a way home through a new understanding of the astral world. This place was a perplexing mystical world, reflecting much of Bali, and the humble sweetness of my Balinese hosts was a continual flowing warmth, while the shaking sessions turned us all into a world-gone-mad. I realised that we were all shaking out the world's madness from within and I dozed off into a blissful slumber, ready to change my life when the new day dawned. Would I be strong enough to cope? Only time would tell. It was time to go back, face my past and stand tall, alone.

The following morning's shake was like it was my last. I pushed hard and again I travelled through a collage of feelings and emotions. I was ready. Breakfast was a sad moment as I had met some amazing people and I wished everyone well. As I was leaving my room, I saw that the entire community had gathered. They formed a circle around me and began to sing. I moved around the group hugging everyone. At the end, Ratu appeared and gave me one more of his incredible hugs. Suddenly and spontaneously, I cried like a baby. It was like a lifetime of pent-up emotion came flooding to the surface. I cried and sobbed for what seemed forever. It was the most beautiful farewell I have ever experienced.

Driving out the gates, I found the past week hard to fathom. At the start, I had been trashed in some morbid nightclub seriously fearing for my well-being and suddenly I was spun one-hundred-and-eighty degrees and following the true essence of my heart. It all seemed so surreal. But I realised an ongoing, highly challenging journey still lay ahead, such was the reality of my life. I had travelled a hard road to get this far and had received such a poignant opportunity.

Returning to the hotel in Kuta, I picked up my records, opening the record cases to see if all was intact. It was like opening a magic chest, my records holding within them the spells of the lower astral field. The smell of stale smoke, ground deep in the slip covers, filled my senses with the memory of a life now well and truly aborted. I closed them, as though closing a casket of the deceased. Carrying them on my journey back to Australia, I felt I was carrying back a life of bittersweet memories — pleasure and pain.

Part Three

18. Highway to hell or stairway to heaven?

RETURNING HOME, A NEW sense of optimism had kindled within, though I still carried the deep scars of a life in the fast lane and the reality of rehabilitation to normality. Living in the West remained a lonely stance. The astral energetic world that had entertained and entrapped me was at the heart of what I was ready to commit to understanding further. I had to discover more if I were to heal and reconnect to myself and life. I had been presented with the gift of shaking. I *needed* to shake now, to become more sensitive and to seek greater insight of this celestial intelligence and only then, I hoped, could life become clearer, enabling me to see and feel the essence of true healing power. Energy — the lower astral field — got me into that mess, and only energy — the higher — could free me of my past deeds.

Why me, when many close to me on the same sorry path had crumbled? Was it my yearning for discovering truth? Deep down, I had always wanted to know the truth behind the power of drugs and their pain. I remember the ashram Balinese telling me that my soul had reincarnated in this life for this type of test.

Excited, I called the practitioner who had initially presented me with this precious gift of opportunity, eager to continue my quest for discovery. I couldn't let the energetic thieves of my soul get a stranglehold on me again. But when I called the healing centre, I was told that the practitioner had moved to England. It was just me in the big smoke, alone with a residual past life ever ready to throw me back into the snake pit. And it didn't take long for a sign of its presence: *sugar!* That impulsive thought once again entered my mind. I realised I had not fought with that thought at all in Bali, but its torment was building in strength and I wasn't sure if I could hold back its force. I knew that once I succumbed to a sugar binge, it would open the gateway and I would be drawn back into the scene looking for stimulation, comfort and familiarity. Shaking helped silence its baiting.

It was time to move beyond the fairytale of Bali. I had a choice — disregard what I was led to believe by my friends in Bali and take medication that would *miraculously* make it all disappear, or trust that there was a subtle intelligence happening within and around me. My experiences were confirmation enough that drugs held a kind of code that tuned me into a new mind-set pattern, changing my very life. I may have called it paranoia; the doctor, anxiety; the priest, possessed; and society, madness. But with all the different labels, one thing was unified — *some* type of energy was communicating a powerful inner message. It was outside my comfort zone, beyond my view of normality and coming from *somewhere*. No one — outside of the people I had so far come across in Bali — could tell me where the dark thoughts were coming from. But society, without knowing exactly how, accepted that drugs bring on despair, misery and darkness.

A higher subliminal intelligence was working within my life — all of humanity's, I believed. I finally had a plausible cause-and-effect answer — a legitimate answer I could truly relate to and not disregard as something imagined. In accepting the astral world in all its loving and destructive mystery, I hoped to return to leading a normal happy life.

And higher intelligence was far from me proclaiming to be talking to UFOs or the Virgin Mother, though I didn't doubt anyone who believed those to be their experiences — especially drug users. This intelligence had worked in changing my mind-set. It had changed the way I thought and acted, and it was not in harmony with how I believed life should be viewed and lived. Driven with a dark motive, encompassing numerous inharmonious repetitive traits, this intelligence continued to dictate certain actions that only led to a place of despair, fear and misery — and progressively, the failure of my body.

As I stood on my balcony gazing out across the city, I could sense the contrasting polarities of the higher and lower vibrational frequencies. *Feel what energy is communicating, Paul.* Society was buzzing its own signature frequency, enticing me and grooming the unsuspecting to desensitise and go full throttle. As well as drug availability, the hypnotic allure of the nocturnal social scene excited the masses, as the arrival of each weekend was a revered moment. Clubs, pubs and bars were society's places of worship — a way to release, relax and change the mind to another frequency. It was a few-drinks-jump from stress to pleasure. Big business even cashed in on the trend to take me unbridled to the unknown, with a plethora of caffeine-packed soft drinks and candy bars almost falling from the heavily packed shelves of petrol stations, supermarkets and corner stores.

Top 40 music was no more about sweet matters of the heart; it was more about soft porn, with female artists dressed like hookers and dancing like strippers. TV programs focused on sex, crime, sick minds and inflated egos, with the only respite being the countless commercials squeezed in to frustrate and salivate, selling the cheapest products — such as premium ice cream, gourmet biscuits and discerning taste chocolate — in the highest costing medium. Computer games were morbid death and destruction, with users skilfully being honed to mastering the lower vibrational techniques of those virtual worlds. And the catwalks — well our *femme fatales* said it all. 'Get them while they're young' — emotionless and waif, sexualised adolescents. Sex and masochism were the lures being flaunted at every corner. Even my 12-year-old niece was a worthy target, with her chosen magazine teaching her how to have the perfect orgasm. People were shitty, paranoid, corrupt and ruthless. I was part of a fast — and sick — society. I certainly was a coherent part of a collective mind.

It no longer surprised me why, here in Australia, the most fortunate country on Earth, we held an unenviable record of high male youth suicide and female attempted suicide. Dysfunction, bi-polar, ADD — the list of labels for tormented minds continued to fill the Sunday papers' health sections. No wonder that mental health was looming as the number one medical issue in the Western world. Finally, things were clearer: *countless sicknesses and one unified source and cure — Energy.* But to the masses, a plethora of new prescriptions with ghastly unpronounceable names *are* the cure. Don't worry about the possible suicidal side effects, if your liver is failing or the possibility that your kidneys could fail, just 'Take this pill, sign here and... next!'

I had to raise my vibration and open my heart. Armed with a few new tools of insight and an abatement of the chronic pain I had now known for too long, shaking and a commitment to seeking new information and understanding was all I had. I was ready to fight pain, sickness and suffering in the most potent and purest way. I had broken not only many social laws over the years, but also other laws of which I was ignorant. I was paying my just dues. Now it was time to become a celestial citizen by way of the universal laws — the true laws and energy would be my redemption. Could I heal myself and regain a sense of optimism for life, health in my body and peace within my mind?

To continue on, I had to journey back. Every wrong turn of the past encompassed a preceding set of choices — high vibrational unity or low vibrational discord. In unravelling and understanding my past choices and their accompanying dynamics, I could make new choices with greater awareness, which would realign me with the harmonious resonance of the now and continue to attune me on the path I was meant to travel — the path of health and happiness. But the voice continued toying with my mind and aggravating my body: *sugar. Feed me you bastard!* Shaking was keeping it at bay, but I could sense that this cumbersome addiction was still running its course for power.

19. Busted!

WITHOUT KNOWING HOW TO SUPPORT myself for the long term, I had to break free of the club scene at any cost. Not long after contacting the clubs to cancel my services, I received a call from a childhood friend who owned a small business. I had worked for him occasionally when his workload was too busy. He asked if I wanted to take over his business, as his focus was now on a new venture. It was the life shift I needed, and I quickly said yes.

The business was placing spotlights above 'For Sale' boards on residential properties around Sydney — a Mr Nobody job and a far cry from the ego-induced work I had been lavishing for so long. The money was excellent and, although it threw me into the gridlock of the city, it was a world away from the club scene and a good first step. But I still carried deep, dark secrets. Anxious and disconnected from everyone, I was out of the frying pan but not the fire.

About a month after arriving home from Bali, I received a call from the woman I had been scoring pounds for. She was in need of another one. I knew it was not conducive anymore to where I wanted to go in life, but I felt some obligation to help her out. After all, it was just a phone call away and it shouldn't cause me any harm. It wasn't about earning $200; it was to help her out. I made a call to my supplier friend. I wasn't prepared to travel across the city, and so we decided to meet at an inner-city petrol station, as we'd done in the past. I collected the $3,000 from the woman and then headed for the rendezvous spot. I pulled into the parking bay of the service station and it was busy with motorists refilling — a perfect spot to remain incognito. The supplier's van pulled up next to my car and we both got out of our cars and began chatting. After about ten minutes, I got back into my car to get the money — ready to deduct my couple-of-hundred dollars — and he got into his. He then got back out and threw the pound onto my lap.

Just at that moment, a man suddenly appeared from nowhere, waving a badge, saying, 'Police. Don't move. You are under arrest!' A moment later, there were about ten plainclothes officers surrounding us and we were instructed to move away from the cars. In my car the officers retrieved a pound of hydro and $3,000. Then they opened the back of his van. They were stunned and started shaking each other's hands congratulating themselves for a job well done. Unloading the contents of the van, they began to place pound after pound onto the parking lot — fifty-something pounds in all, a stack of cash, and seven mobile phones. Young motorists pulling into the service station looked on in amazement, with a few whistling and yahooing.

One of the officers came over to me and said that it was my unlucky day. My friend had been under surveillance for quite some time and I was the one who had to take the fall with him. 'You were in the wrong place, at the wrong time, with the wrong guy.' The police could see from the single pound in my car and the money that I was only getting one pound. We were taken back to police headquarters in the city, where we were questioned. I was charged with the pound of marijuana and the cash, and then allowed to leave to attend local court in a month. I was fined $500. My supplier friend was held in custody.

I remembered old-man Putu in Bali telling me that the energy will cut the past and that it will always give me the best. 'Energy very clever,' I remembered him saying. I embraced this predicament in the way I should have earlier, when I had the chance to decline the woman's request for another pound — trusting the power of the astral. It was my first test, of which I was told would come often to tempt me back to the old ways. I wanted to say no, but I gave in to her needs — her lower astral needs. And I paid the price and mentally marked it down as one-nil in favour of the visitors. I didn't really care about being busted. What I accepted was the intelligence of this power working through my life now in a positive way. I had learnt a powerful lesson.

The way my friend appeared when he did, offering me a new job, taking me away from the club scene, so too was my cessation of drugs the work of the higher astral. I'd been involved with drugs for so many years because I was a great tool of the lower astral and I was 'allowed' to continue on. I remembered Ratu's talk and how he said it was easy to get what we want for the mind because there was so much darkness in the world. But suddenly, with a shift in my awareness, the higher astral cut it from my life, almost immediately.

I had been caught and charged with drugs as a teen, just as I was entering a lower astral life of drugs and partying — a definite warning. And the next time I would be caught, some twenty years later, was at the end, when the energy was guiding me back — when I was ready to be guided back. Scoring for that woman was easy money every now and again. To keep it going would certainly have been counterproductive to me on many levels. The time was decided by another force. It was a force that was intent on changing my life for the better, sooner rather than later, and I wasn't keen to flirt with any more tests.

20. Medicine Crow

I ENJOYED MY NEW JOB, placing lights on auction boards, but feeling alone was still tormenting me. I didn't really have anything to do with anyone down at the beach anymore, finding that I really didn't resonate with the path my old friends were on. My lesson, my test with marijuana, was sobering, but it soon left me disillusioned. The past was being cut from my life, from my own choosing and the energy's, but I was left with a void, inside an empty person. Without the past, I felt like an isolated vessel, floating aimlessly around the city. I began to withdraw further, questioning all the negativity surrounding me. It was as though I really didn't fit in to society anymore. It was like I was suspended between two worlds, many times thinking, *What's the use of transforming myself when I'm surrounded by all that I'm trying to break free of? I'm a lonely figure in a false society.*

I shared with a couple of close mates the shaking practice and they laughed at me, saying that I had lost it and that I needed to get out more and enjoy myself. That thought did enter my mind, but socialising — the city way — scared me. I just rode my pushbike and swam laps of the beach as recreational pursuits — solo pursuits. Even my lighting job was just me in my car, and in and out of a property before anyone had the chance to get too close. No one was interested in shaking, energy, and least of all astral intelligence. It was just me. I was shaking on my own as often as I could, but I couldn't reach the intensity that I did in Bali. My ears continued to leak for three months, a reminder of my time in Bali. They eventually healed without any further problems. But Bali was beginning to seem like a distant dream. I tried to stay positive, but without the support of others on the same astral path, it was difficult. I was alone and working with some serious history that was far from healed.

One day I turned up to a property, the last of the day, and

went about installing the lighting equipment. I knocked on the front door to ask the vendor for access to a power point. The man who answered was a foreigner, draped in tribal jewellery and a colourful poncho, cordoned with ornate trinkets. He had a thick American accent and deep, almost black eyes. Looking at him, his heritage seemed part African, and the way his hair fell long and straight, part Indian. Inviting me in to complete the job, the smell of burnt incense was like it was ingrained into the walls, and his home was decorated with native North American Indian artefacts. I immediately felt captivated with his collection of drums, feathers, furs and knick-knacks. His home felt powerful, as did his presence. Paying compliments to his unique decor, I asked if he were a healer.

'Healer is a very loose term these days. I don't heal. I help, because no one can heal anyone else. But with the right help, all things are possible.' He introduced himself as Medicine Crow: 'But you may call me Cary.' I was quite attentive to all the fascinating pieces, which completely furbished his home, when Cary asked if I would like something to drink. I said yes — normally saying no — and as he went to the kitchen I completed the installation. He returned with a cup of cold tea of some sort and we sat on his couch, which was covered in a colourful tribal coverlet.

'Your home reminds me of a place I've just returned from in Bali.'

'Ah, Bali; it's a very sacred and powerful place in our world,' he replied, as he eased himself into the backrest.

I continued by sharing the incredible information I was given regarding the energetic world of the astral plane and the shaking practice. I felt some trepidation to divulge too much about my shady past; after all, I was there for work. But as the conversation opened up, I felt safe to do so in Cary's presence. It felt strange that we were here, now, speaking of such matters. I said that I now have some type of vocation in trying to discover more of this incredible world and use the knowledge to heal myself.

Cary, in a very patient manner, took a slow, deep breath: 'Not long ago, here in Australia, a huge storm filled a dry lake in the centre of the continent, which had been exhausted for many years. Within a few days, countless flocks of birds flew thousands of kilometres to the lake for the first time ever in their lives, from all corners of the country. Man, how did they know the storm had arrived, that the lake was full, and how did they know where it was? If you were to tell society that you were given a message from the universe, informing you that a storm had just arrived thousands of kilometres away and you were leaving, with no map, to go and enjoy a lake you knew nothing about, that has been empty for years but now is full... you would be chastised as a fool! But we witness this miracle of higher energetic intelligence in nature — and what do most people do? Turn to the next page of the newspaper without giving it another thought.

'Paul, energetic intelligence is nature's birthright. It's just that poor ol' humanity has decided to shut itself off from the universe — and actually travel blind on its own. We're livin' in a time, Man, where the blind are truly leading the blind. Every person's aim in this life should be to reconnect to their true nature because, by reconnecting, you reconnect to who you really are.'

'And who am I?' I asked, not in any way trying to sound a smart ass.

'Well I can tell you who you are not; you're not a cool city DJ or a lighting installer. They're just masks. You're a soul searching for itself through all those images you cover yourself with. And that is what the ego is. It is the mind identifying with the body. Those images people cling to are all BS. And to know who you are, you have to know what you are.'

With a deep American voice that commanded respect, and not from fear of strength, but somehow resonating with a powerful clarity that held my attention, he continued: 'You are a walking ball of energy that is connected to the cosmos — literally. Every vibrating atom is resonating at a certain frequency, vibrating out, from within, invisibly — from all over your body. Try and picture yourself as a walking antenna, with your portals, which are specific energetic gateways, or chakras, unconsciously emanating a type of telepathy about yourself and picking up all sorts of information about those — and all — around you. The chakras are a very established and accepted part of both Indian spirituality and Ayuvedic medicine but, in the West, they're more like a cool alternative way to pamper oneself. No one really wants to unearth the depths of it all. Just get them fine-tuned off the guy advertising in the back of the TV mag! Aligned and off you go! But anyway... the aura is the overall energetic vibration of your chakras and colour spectrum visible to the trained eye. Your aura says a lot about who you are. It's your invisible, universal ID.

'Look around, Man. Our crazy world is now a manifestation of not knowing anything other than the prison of the mind. And the prison of the mind is not who you are, even though it will create an image of who it wants you to be. Paul, energy *is* intelligent. It is information for us to tap into. Like the birds, on masse, flying to the centre of this amazing continent, it's a universal law. But humanity is so far removed from its higher source at the moment. The masses aren't even aware that they are connecting to the lower either, dude. But people *are* beginning to realise something ain't right in the world. Many things ain't right in the world now.'

I was beginning to enjoy Cary's tone. He had that African-American flare, quite animated and real but very grounded in his delivery. With another relaxed pause, holding a moment's silence with a type of reverence, he went on. 'The human chakra system is a series of energetic vortexes, seven major ones in all, that spin as centres of activity from strategic points from the body. These pathways correlate to different bodily functions and are also our link to the higher self. They call it the astral self in Bali. My ancestors named it the spirit world. Development and function of the chakras corresponds to major areas of a person's life, such as survival, reproduction, ego, love, communication, perception and knowledge. Should the chakra system become inhibited in its growth, through trauma for example, one's perceptual filter is a direct influence of their chakras' state of health, and how you view yourself and the world around you could be the difference between joy and suffering. And that perception is influenced by the astral dimensions.'

Pausing again, as he sipped on his tea, it was as if he had all the time in the world. Then he slowly placed his cup back onto the coaster and continued, like this was knowledge he was surprised no one took seriously. 'Traumatisation disrupts social growth and weakens your defences against the astral world. Traumatisation retards the body's vibration and places you on a congruent path to long-term suffering.'

I thought, *no wonder life's a challenge; all this astral knowledge really is a science — a complicated science.* Then jokingly I said, 'There was a time as a young boy when I always wondered what the yellow paint splashed around the picture of Jesus was.'

Cary, with a slight chuckle, said, 'Dude, we're all splashed with the same brush, although not many have had the same influence as that picture. That *paint* is the aura, which I'm sure you realised. Like I just said, the aura is an antenna, sending and receiving signals. You need to ensure that the energy you are receiving is nurturing, clean and resonating at a higher frequency. Stay clear of anyone or anything that stimulates any channels you are trying to close. That energy would be from certain people or places — and items.'

'I've seen quite a lot of healers in the past who couldn't really mend me, but no doubt working with those people would have been nurturing and clean wouldn't it? I've always taken it for granted that healers must hold some power to remain grounded and healthy.'

'When you first arrived, I said to you that I don't heal, I help.

Depending on the type of treatment, practitioners can and do absorb other people's negative energy, unless they have a very strong resonance — all day, every day. Many practitioners anoint themselves as healers, yet are unaware and naïve to the *incredible* forces they are playing with, so far as keeping themselves energetically clean. Energy interplays and if you are striving for clarity within your chakras, whoever places their hands upon you is placing the history of those with whom they have worked. Keeping energetically clean really needs to be an individual responsibility. Paul, with all due respect, if I knew a *healer* was about to channel energy onto me, after just working on a guy with a past like yours, I'd end up being painted with your stuff, not cleaned of mine. It's as simple as that. And if I'm the last client of the day, well, say no more.

'We all have the ability to connect to the spirit world. Dude, we are part of the spirit world, but who knows what level of the astral *they* are channelling. They'll say it's the highest of course, but hey, they're not going to get you to sign a disclaimer that there may be a chance some foreign entity could jump on board! I tell you, Paul, if anyone advertises themselves saying that they will heal you with their own powers, put your wallet back in your pocket and run.'

'I take it that you're not a healer, then?'

'Well, you're right. I'm not a healer and don't advertise myself as one. I'm not someone who accepts money for holistic services. But if I did accept money from you, it would have to be clear that there is no dependency. I'm not dependent on you to pay my rent and if you become dependent on me for help, that doesn't help anybody. I have no thought of material gain from you. I'm simply a guy with information that not too many people want to take seriously. True healers live in sacred spaces within themselves and offer that channel as a source of cleansing, and do so coming from a life of complete service to the heavens and humanity — all day, every day of their lives. And I can't think of any that dwell in big cities.

'I know only you can heal yourself. And I know I haven't compromised the good work you're doing on yourself by placing you in a position where I may infuse you with past treatments of other people's energy I may have taken on board — because I'm not channelling. We're exchanging energy, which is what being human is, unless you live in a cave. But I'm not channelling energy. Not too many people can truly channel or move energy while working on people and remain an innocent bystander. And those who *can* channel *healing* energy don't advertise their gifts in the local mags in the healing section, right next to the escort section. A good question to ask a *healer* is, "Have you been healed?"'

There was once a time when I would have thought that this guy was a full-on day-tripper, but with life unfolding the way it had been, his words were certainly full-on, but far from tripping-out. He made a lot of sense. He asked if I would like some more tea and I accepted, enjoying this opportunity to delve into the astral world. Since Bali, it was like it was non-existent here in the city — well, the higher astral anyway.

'We live in the information age, Paul,' said Cary, relaxing back into the sofa. 'Unfortunately, most are embracing technology as gospel. But there is greater information, which should be where the collective focus is. It too moves through the air, interacting with everyone and everything around, but it's out of the conditioned perception of the majority of people's five senses. It's intelligent energy, and it's always available to share its secrets should one have the gift to really see. It sounds as though you had to taste its darker polarity to open your eyes in awakening the storyteller. How wide your eyes are open determines what you can see. What you give off energetically can be read by others and vice versa.'

With a wry smile, I replied, 'That makes sense, after one of *those* weekends, people would literally cross the street to avoid coming into contact with me.'

'Of course, they inherently tuned *themselves* into the energetic vibration you were emanating at the time, thus tuning themselves out. Bad vibes, Man, can clear a packed room. People *do* react to energy without consciously knowing the depths of the order. We all exchange the conditioned energetic information we are living, filtered through our chakras. If you spend enough time with someone or a group, you will influence each other with the energetic state you are at. That's why it's so important to continually remain grounded and centred. *The Vedic* scriptures of the Hindus you spent time with in Bali are thousands of years old. Their scriptures refer to the energetic dynamics of the chakras, but, nowadays, like most scriptures, especially in the West, true understanding has given way to parlance.

'When you engage someone, your optical senses send and receive messages, thus forming an interactive connection and/or an evaluation of that person — and vice versa. A total two-way harmony is what a true connection is. It is a visual, invisible connection of our souls. If there is harmony within yourself, you are really communicating, because it can only then come from your heart. If there is no harmony, what looks like communication is actually a subtle game of dysfunctional energies interacting. Together with the aura's ability to also sense and convey information, words are the least important tool we communicate with. It's what we sense with our aura and eyes. Being disconnected with life and oneself, distorted information is sent and received. At times, information is over-perceived, such as: "They think I'm this" or "They are sensing that about me." It's that latent field repelling and attracting you to certain people, while you are talking.'

Cary paused for a moment, took another sip of his tea, and then ran his fingers through his long hair, pulling it back behind his neck and tying it with a coloured band that was tied around his wrist. Sitting forward and looking more intently at me, he continued on. 'And that field is a mirror. You may feel hatred, or jealousy, or whatever, when you look into someone's eyes. This is another one of the mysteries of energetic intelligence. If you are in a fragile and disconnected state, whatever *your* blockages and darkness are, those inner feelings project onto a certain person or people, only to see your own dark reflection back in *their* eyes. It's not that you hate them — it's that you hate you, dude. Or you feel jealous about a trait in that person that you wish *you had.*

'The energy distorts with whatever negative opinions you have of others. The pain and weakness, or even strengths and confidence, you see in others is too painful to acknowledge in yourself. Your condemnation, discrimination and apathy are your own reflective blocks in the eyes of others. Disconnected from life and ungrounded from yourself, you form a negative opinion of that person or simply avoid them so as not to ignite that invisible muddy signal, hurtling back like radar from that certain person. To coin a phrase, you have clouded vision. And that is when you know that you don't know who you are. And with so many people disconnected from themselves now, communication is empty words laced with all sorts of funky vibes bouncing back and forth. When you accept others unconditionally, then you accept yourself totally.'

'Whoa,' I murmured. There was no doubt that the window to my inner essence was covered in a dull and heavy shroud and the wrong messages were coming out and bouncing back. My eyes had lost that high vibrational sparkle and no matter how hard I tried to paint a facade of peace and happiness, the information filtering my judgment was anything but. 'Yeah,' I said, 'I've seen that energy in all its glory on countless reality TV shows. You know, the camera panning right into the eyes and confronting questions being asked, hoping to get an eye-emotional reaction. Why is that?'

'You tell me, Paul. Ask yourself: Are we supposed to accept their TV-exposed blockages as their stuff and remain in a false sense of detached empowerment? Would a despondent reply make us feel that *we are* normal, it's okay and that everyone reacts with a twitch, an aggressive glare or a teary gaze? Does our deepest knowing and search for *truth* magnetise us to the strong ones who seem to have found that elusive state of centredness? Or do we accept them as they are, without any yearning or judgment? You need to see within yourself what it is that attracts or repels you. Begin with energy every time. That is the key.'

It was now nightfall, and it seemed that we had been talking for hours. It was an amazing experience and I acknowledged to myself that Cary was another gift from the universe to help me on my way. I said I would like to provide the lighting installation to him for free for his time. He raised his hand and placed it on my shoulder.

'Paul, this is my gift to you. You have a strong desire for discovering the truth and that discovery will heal you. That's a brave act, Man. You are taking control of your life. Besides, this is not my house, I am renting,' he said, smiling. 'I was given notice to move out once my lease expired and now I am heading back to the States. It is time to move on. But I appreciate your offer of the complementary installation.'

Yet another person entering my life with guidance and slipping back out with no way to meet again, I thought.

As I was leaving, Cary shook my hand and, with a parting piece of wisdom, concluded our conversation: 'Paul, do you place these lights all over town?'

'Yes.'

'Use your job now as a metaphor for your life — spreading light.'

'Thanks Cary,' my eyes finding a clear connection to hold his parting goodbye.

'Stay strong, brother.'

21. Snakes and ladders

THE SPONTANEITY OF THAT ENCOUNTER with Cary came right when I needed it. Some of what he said, I'd heard from other healers or read about. But since I'd been working with the dynamics of the astral, and vibrational information, it suddenly resonated with me. I was feeling the information, instead of simply taking it into my mind, like I had in the past. I didn't feel so alone in the city anymore, despite knowing I may never meet Cary again. People were out there, following their own truth, and I accepted that I needed to process a lot of negativity, even if it meant enduring a rocky road of isolation, pain and doubt. That evening, after shaking and meditation, I relaxed. Like a jigsaw puzzle painstakingly being pieced together to reveal its identity, I began to correlate all the incredible information I had received. I had a map and I now had a way of reading it. The pieces were falling into place.

Due to major anxiety in my life till I was sixteen, my chakra system had not developed appropriately. I had been continually exposed to the violent fighting between my parents for as long as I can remember. This chronic disturbance in my developing chakra system — all lower frequency trauma — tempered the initial gateway for the dark energy to enter into my life and express itself through me. Trauma weakened my defences by inhibiting the healthy development of my energetic body — my link to the heavens. With a long childhood of extreme fear, I was being 'groomed', energetically, for bigger things. This is why it felt right and seemed easy for me to indulge in and gravitate towards the lifestyle I did. From my 'let's go' bravado with marijuana at seventeen, I had a predisposed alignment with the real energy behind Sex, Drugs and Techno. It was a connection to the lower astral frequency, established via the legacy of my violent childhood, and this repression was certain to expose itself at some point in my life.

From my traumatic childhood, my life became a series of events that were sequenced with sheer precision — all unconsciously. My parents' divorce at sixteen meant an end to the fighting and fear, but at seventeen I began smoking marijuana habitually. At twenty-eight, I tired of daily marijuana smoking and, within a month of breaking that cycle, ecstasy and serious partying entered my life. When the fast lane became overpowering, sugar became the vice to entice. The lower astral wove its consecutive servitude like clockwork, needing a new manipulative alignment to keep it empowered — and me enslaved. Years of feeding my body drugs and alcohol had conditioned my system to its weekly, energetic fixes. But it was slowly breaking down my body's defences — spiritually, emotionally, mentally and physically. Sugar as the new vice ensured this energy maintained its power over me, keeping me sedated from my true potential. This low vibrational intelligence needed to keep me in *its* power to keep its own destructive power.

Once this energy alignment continued permeating through me, via my destructive partying lifestyle, the astral intelligence changed my mind-set. It had found a complementary resonance, and its manifestations slowly grew into darker, more anti-harmony actions. The only outcome from this domino effect of 'traumatised chakras' and 'alignment to the lower astral frequency' could be misery, pain and an eventual demise. I became a living, precipitous channel for this vibration — and its dark maxim — to work through me. Coming down was simply a stepping stone of this energy. Entropy was the crescendo.

The ultra-low vibration of drugs aligned me with like-minds. A certain camaraderie was shared with people on the same path. I emitted the energetic feeling/desire (vibration) and found 'harmony' with like-minds who resonated the same astral chord of Sex, Drugs and Techno. I bonded and felt right with that crowd. The crowds were straight/gay/mixed, and with those unknown faces along side of me, I found some subliminal belonging/connection through a web of like-music, like-drugs and like-clubs. That is why at a huge dance party I felt so much sensual and loving energy when the collective mass was united and peaking on E from around midnight to 4 a.m.

But the reality was that once a dance party crowd began to come down from its peak, the entire room was connecting to the real information of that plane. It was *always* a dreary, draining, sick and fragile experience. Coming down was *the sign* of a lower frequency alignment. I would feel that energy's manifestations, such as shitty, depressed, sexual, self-defeating and negative.

During my early days with dance parties, love seemed to be the feeling in the air early in the night, but, over time, as more and more people abused drugs, the energy of love turned into a more sexual, lustful energy. The masses were all falling into that darker world. The illusion was no longer needed. The weirdest aspect was that, no matter how uncomfortable or twisted the end of a big night's comedown was, or how disconnected I began to feel, I was ready to do it all again the following week. The energy seductively kept me wanting to taste the power of the heart again and again. The cycle was well set in motion through the yearning of love/oneness/a buzzing feeling. Maya!

After prolonged overstimulation of my system, people would avoid me, sensing my sleaziness, heaviness, aggression, desperation and sadness — *and* vice versa. It was like I had a sign hanging from my neck reading: *'Avoid like the plague!'* The complexities of me being a beautiful human were being mashed up in a lower astral blender through drugs and partying. The dark aspects of life were encroaching and rising to the surface — in me and in those around me. We were on the same scattered path, sending out all sorts of crazy profaneness, and dragging all on a one-way spiral down. I thought drugs were okay and were actually connecting me to some *guarded* Godly place. Now that *is* where madness shone! It was such a converse game — a clever game of snakes and ladders!

Eventually, the deceptive buzz of drugs couldn't hide the fact that I was a mess, no matter how much I thought I was emanating love. One moment I could walk up to a complete stranger, on E, and begin to passionately kiss, like long lost lovers, whereas later on, when we were both coming down from the same drug and resonating in true accordance of the drug's dark, low frequency, we *would* avoid each other like the plague. This was all in the space of a couple of hours. After years of consuming and connecting, and with a childhood of low vibrational trauma, I became so conditioned to that lower frequency that drugs were no longer required to keep me there and I lived each day emanating a — conscious — heavy low vibration. Before long, I felt that the darkness inside *was me!* My connection was well and truly secured.

Being in a continual interactive energy exchange became tormenting, with a steady decline into further fear, isolation and negativity. I tended to avoid many situations in life, such as catching up with friends and family. I avoided certain places, fearing an uncomfortable outcome from any interaction. I was *living* a universal message of low vibrational darkness, which continued to pour in like a virus and out like some type of stale scent through the air.

And when it was time to seek help, I simply turned up to the door of countless healers with the dependent energy of 'YOU fix ME!', never contemplating that only I could heal myself. Aligning myself with those who I thought were powerful people, because they had a nice certificate hanging from their wall or claimed they could free my soul of a thousand past lives, door-knocking kept me from taking control of my own life. I'd been to countless healers, with many claiming to channel energy or to clear blocks, but not one amounted to anything other than pampering.

I could see how too many games were allowed to play with too many healers, such as sex, competition, judgment — the ego.

Their personal energy field wasn't vibrationally strong enough. At times, negativity would fill the air and begin a mind game, wasting my time, money and opportunity to grow. But it was a lottery out there.

I thought of all the suspect healers I had encountered. At the Satsung classes, the teacher had to leave because he slept with one of the students who afterwards freaked out and left. Then the guy who replaced him suffered a brain tumour and was paralysed completely down one side of his body, even though he was telling me he knew the way to live free. I couldn't understand how a man in his thirties on such a devoted spiritual path could end up like that. I saw a chiropractor who rotated four patients at a time and simply stuck a few electric suction cups to my back and left me alone for the rest of the treatment. He gave me more face-to-face attention when preparing my bill and arranging my return appointment for more of the same treatment. One healer told me he could fix my bad back by massaging my coccyx — from inside my rectum. I declined, but I'm sure I would have received plenty of attention during that treatment! One therapist I knew of only treated women by helping them release deep inner blocks by massaging muscles deep inside their vaginas with his fingers.

And kahoona! I couldn't think of a single man who, lying naked on his back with legs spread open, having enough oil lathered on him to cook chips for an army and covered with only a sheet while a twenty-something woman massaged his thighs, stomach, all over, would have his mind solely on the therapeutic and holistic power of one of those treatments. I finished one of those sessions and thought, *That was one kahoona of an experience. I'll probably need another one.* Other treatments weren't so provocative; one practitioner told me that if I got out of bed each day and placed both feet on the ground at the same time that would fix me: 'Try that, and that will be $50, thanks.'

Simply surrendering myself to any alternative health practitioner was not a remedy for healing. I needed a healer who was not sick on a deeper level from absorbing other people's negative energy; who acted whole (unlike, 'do as I say, not as I do'); who was committed to the very best service of each client (not a money spinner of four per hour); who didn't perform questionable treatments that left too much for the imagination to run wild (under the heading 'healing'); who was incorruptible from energetic mind games (be it sexual or ego); and who resonated with a presence of love and absolute clarity. And out of all the healers, how could I tell who was who, energetically? Finding a legitimate practitioner, who absolutely knew the way for me to heal and who truly lives the path of his or her ancient teachings, coming from a sacred space, was to discover a rare jewel hidden within the vast and varied healers out there. I thought of only one... Ratu Bagus.

22. The science of wisdom

MY REALISATIONS WOULD NOT SIT WELL with the mainstream consensus, even though well-known authors such as Deepak Chopra and Fritjof Capra promote the knowledge of universal law. Society accepts energetic intelligence to a degree. Some of these remain in the socially accepted and collective experience category, including gut feelings, synchronicity, sexual attraction, good vibes/bad vibes, and even the biological functioning of the body and nature. Others are outside of the normal thinking/behaviour mind-set.

The Sex, Drugs and Techno scene was an incredible platform for energy to communicate and integrate. And I had to feel somewhat grateful in a sorry way that the energy of drugs had hit me with all it had. There only could have been one of two outcomes — fail ignorant or win aware. In accepting, as do Eastern and tribal cultures, that energetic intelligence is a very real part of life itself and exists everywhere and influences everyone — whether it's someone holding a spear or wearing a suit — the mainstream West would tell me otherwise: 'No break-through; go see the doctor!'

Since the West has shaped this loving, peaceful, honest and connected world of mine, and since all those in power are working for the greater good of humankind and the environment, and not embarking on conquests of rape and pillage, and since it is evolving into a utopia I'd love to leave to my grandkids, well then maybe the West knows best! After all, it was Western colonialism that stripped the tribal heathens of their spiritual cultures, claiming they were devil worshipers, even though countless tribal cultures honoured — and understood — all levels of the spirit world, which was a world away from what the West was forcing upon them.

I pulled a book from my collection of esoteric/self-help titles.

It was, *Hands of Light*, by Barbara Ann Brennan. A bestseller of the late '80s, it was a type of reference, helping people who consider themselves aspirants to better physical, psychological and spiritual health. She developed her own conclusions as a model for spiritual healing work. I found it fascinating to read that book again, many years after I first purchased it. There was a suggestion by a physicist, Jack Sarfatti, that 'things' and events are correlated on a plane of reality above our own, with things in that plane connected to an even higher one.

What I found most intriguing was that the author dedicated a section of the book to the reality of the healer getting sick themselves from healing people. If the healer fails to 'clean' their own energetic field, they will get sick because the healer uses their own energy field as their instrument. But, with all the healers out there, opening themselves up to the astral world — in all of its light and dark frequencies — who really can be completely assured that some darker vibrational energy doesn't enter into a session from either the healer or the patient? Ms Brennan says that the healer must be aware that it is the healing of the soul they are working with. With all I was *now* discovering, I couldn't help but think that if humanity continues to place its power into another person's hands for the liberation of its soul, then our planet will remain in a needy, victimised state.

Like all the books I have read, none were willing or able to delve deeper into the darker realms of the astral world, and provide an explanation as to the origins of sickness, darkness and chaos, or how we humans are guided, misled and abused by this vibrational force. I was now certain that the liberation of my soul could/would only come from *my own* awareness of the astral world.

Delving a little further into the possibility of shaking being a science, I *was* intrigued as to how shaking could raise one's vibration. With my mind still curious for understanding, I sought information. I found that shaking as a way to heal is steeped in history, from the ancient Greeks and many tribal communities. There were even modern vibrational healing apparatuses for sick patients, and the Russians have used vibrational medicine for cosmonauts and Olympic athletes. One science report stated that scientists have found ways to shake viruses to death with laser pulses tuned to the right frequency but, being such a new frontier, science has not yet had sufficient time to prove itself. The article also claimed that it is unlikely that viruses will develop resistance to mechanical shaking, as they do to drugs.

I could see how Ratu's modern-day shaking, although steeped in history, was probably linked to the ancient tribes-people, rather than some vibrational healing bed or ultrasound device that may be just over the horizon. From my experiences in Bali, I knew that healing my sickness, attachments, past traumas and negative alignments could only take place by raising my overall vibration — not just treating sick cells by a machine. Ratu's practice required *me* to process the negativity within me — by shaking. Shaking would instill a true understanding of my sickness and my life, and heal my past by moving me into a higher vibration overall. And as I continued to seek that golden bridge of science — how intelligence influences oscillations, amplitudes and wavelengths, and how vibrational frequencies connect to the astral dimensions — I realised that science has not yet reached that point of understanding.

I was obtaining a lot of incredible information from some incredible people, who all lived by what science was trying to uncover. It was all making complete sense, relating it to my experiences and what I was witnessing around me. I took solace from Cary's encounter at a time when I was struggling to maintain my focus, trusting that I had to weather the initial setbacks of isolation and fear. I had to trust that the energy would give me the very best if I honour it, and trust that I was turning towards a new phase in my life. But one day 'it' hit me — hard. The words of Ratu came flooding back: 'You have to feel the energy.' I was gaining an understanding of all that I was seeking, and I was becoming receptive and sensitive to the dynamics of energy, yet had I really *felt* all of what I was taking in?

Obviously not! The need for sugar had returned and this time something wanted my attention and wasn't letting up till it had what it desired — total control and destruction of my life force. *Knowing is not healing! I have to feel this energy! I have to stand and face its dominance and servitude!* The only way now was to about-face and look the power of the lower astral world in the eye.

23. The devil in disguise

SUGAR HAD BECOME THE PRIMARY HABIT that tormented me. I could not go a day without stopping at a cake shop, corner store, petrol station or supermarket to fill myself with sweets. I would impulsively ingest muffins, breakfast cereal, chocolate bars — anything with sugar in it. I would pour sweet after sweet into myself until I was sick. Even when it got to the state of knowing that to succumb and gratify my/its luscious desires would cripple me with chronic anxiety (paranoia/fear/ isolation), and the disconnected social baggage which accompanies it, it didn't matter. I was hooked, like heroin. The carrot on the stick was momentary gratification, as the sweetness saturated my taste buds, and momentary peace. But that fleeting moment soon passed, in an instant altering — further — the dynamics of my energetic being. As I ate my way through sugar, sugar was slowly eating away at me.

My mind had decided that it would continue to manipulate me with its own agenda of gluttony and social sedation, so much so that I was literally a puppet on a string. 'It's just sugar for God sake!' I used to moan. I noticed that with the arrival of each craving, it first began with an impulsive thought: *Let's stop and get a muffin.* That automatically sent an energised signal to my stomach, which began to churn and give rise to an uncom-fortable, urgent feeling, which only ceased when I succumbed to the craving, appeasing the energy within. The low vibrational party was not meant to end. I was ready to dawn a new life but this power inside me was nothing short of quicksand — actually quick-sugar. The game was still in favour of the visitors. Some Godly place *was* looking over me because if I had tried heroin, I certainly would have been dead by now. But I was addicted... to sugar of all things.

To move forward I would have to feel this energy in a way I

had been avoiding for so long. In fact, sugar was the end zone. What I would have to feel is this energy's lineage, right back to my childhood. Sugar was simply one of many tarnished layers I had covered myself with. Every day, I had to choose between something that would give me relief and a fake pleasure in the moment — and pain later — or something that would challenge my comfort zone but continually take me to a better place within myself. It was a shadowy affirmation and all I had was a new way of looking at life and approaching my pain — via energy — which I trusted was the only way out. I held onto that belief, knowing deep down that my positive determination would light the path for me to tread. Going down, part of the burnout statistics, was not an option. 'Energy,' I would continue commanding. 'Look for it, Paul. The answers are always in front of us,' I remember James saying. To truly heal myself, I first had to understand myself and my state of being by stepping into a world unknown to most and outside of the domain of society's perception — and acceptance. It was time to feel — really feel. I had to rise above the serpent's strangle.

Fighting my inner demon was to be truly loving myself, even though expressing love was something I could not ever recall doing, least of all to myself. I realised that it was love I had been searching for my whole life. Love within my family was replaced by fighting, and consuming drugs, alcohol, sex and sugar was my way of trying to fill the love lacking inside of me. Every gratuitous act represented a false sense of self-nurturing, fruitlessly trying to fill what had never been there. The delusional love of ecstasy offered me the feeling of love growing from within, becoming one with the crowd. Now was the time to reclaim that most powerful of emotions. Each time I had a mind-body craving (sugar desire), I was intent on exposing the vulnerability of this energy, which was suffocating the energy of my heart. I trusted that I possessed the game's axiom and now it was my opportunity to turn the tables.

'Feel the energy, Paul.' Tuning in to my mind-body connection when it was time to reach for the sweets, my mind had indicated it was time to feed the need. My heart was yearning and the lower astral plane needed its fix and confirmation of my servitude. Instead of entering into compulsive mode, I held off on the act for a moment and noticed what was happening to me: *Okay, the thought is not going anywhere — feed me now!* For a moment, the monkey-mind had to wait because I was out-manoeuvring it from what I hoped was a higher helping hand, deep within.

It was all about the physical craving: 'FEEL IT!' Actually feeling and getting in touch with it churning away in me was uncomfortable. I felt it slowly getting stronger until it felt unbearable. My restless mind tried to overrule the preposterously agitating game I was playing with it, and persistently sought a submissive route away from the torment. All I had to do was reach for the sweets! Just holding off and feeling it build was becoming too much to bear, but that holding and witnessing of my mind-body reaction was the act that I was seeking. I was finally facing my demon.

The longer I sat and abstained, the stronger the craving became. It started to frustrate me, beyond compare, to the point of agony. *This is it, Paul, a major breakthrough. Come on!* I sat with the agony and embraced it — almost to tears. I could feel the shattering of the lower vibrational field. My true self was breaking out to be let free to move into the higher vibrational universe, to move me into a higher quality of life. I was not only exercising my inner strength, but also exorcising the dark spirit living through me. Now I was following my heart, not my head.

For the first time, probably ever, I was feeling my true inner power eager to enter my life, through the painful separation of abstinence. My craving(s) — Maya — continued to throw a huge smokescreen across my perception of pure potentiality, with the illusion so strong and real that that energy ruled. My corrupted mind was my enemy. It was beyond dysfunctional; it was intent on destroying me.

Trying to draw power back from this force, my state of addictive ransom was a powerful blessing in disguise because I had felt — albeit negative — a massive amount of energy flowing through me. In a veritable paradox, my craving was ignited by the agitation of want. My true self was the same agitation, but needing discipline. I always chose the easy, dark route of appeasing that weakness, never understanding that power and weakness — the dualism of light and dark — were one and the same. Life and the entire universe is built on the law of opposites (night/day, hot/cold, good/bad). One could not exist without the balance of the other. In accepting this law, I accepted that every person has God and the devil residing in them. I had to balance these resistant forces by maintaining focus. The choice was always mine.

The random distress that a sugar craving had over me wouldn't be beaten in a day or probably even a month. I was well versed with partying stop/starts. Now understanding what was happening energetically, I had a technique that was so simple it wasn't really even a technique. Just don't do it! It was exercising the discipline of will, which I had never challenged. I had had a strong will for selfish desires, and look where that had led me! I had found another chink in the lower astral's armour.

To be aware of the power game of my addiction was to be aware of the simplicity of its rule. I finally understood how, through traumatised chakras, I would always make the wrong — blinded — choices. Through my weak-willed choices every day, I was feeding a force that would continue to grow in strength. My yearning for love was replaced with a false desire for stimulation of the senses, which continued to numb out the pain of my childhood trauma. Light and dark were simply the consequence of my choice of 'Yes!' or 'No!' If something could drive my actions so powerfully and destructively, rebalancing myself naturally would turn that power around to impel me to a new healthy and happy path. I simply had to acknowledge my need to feel, and not connect to the weaker choice of want.

Over the next few months, blocks were rising and looking for a release. Sometimes, I lacked the strength in that moment, and the pain of separation became too great. I would reach for a raisin and cinnamon muffin. Although not losing it completely was a heart-felt sign that I was gaining in strength, I was failing a battle, but slowly winning the war. I had a lifetime of weak-willed choices and I wasn't superman. I just had to continue to put in a super effort — get knocked down, and get straight back up. It was that painful separation that I had to slowly endure. It was the mental fight I had to turn up to — alone, every day — in breaking through a forty-year lineage of addictions and family trauma. There was no time, room nor advantage blaming, what-iffing or dwelling, becoming another self-pitied victim. As my solicitor said to me prior to my recent court appearance: 'You did what you did and these are the cards you've been dealt. So play your best hand with what you've got.'

Pain clouded my belief in myself at times, but putting my best hand forward, the game became clearer for what it was and that inner, painful churning feeling was an initial weak-mind smoke-screen fighting with my true self ready and waiting to shine. What seemed intense initially, slowly began to give rise to feelings of triumph and real high-on-life experiences. Sitting with the pain, and building resilience, was tapping me into the higher vibrational vortex of my power and the only way to taste it was to do the hard yards. It was just like any sport... no pain, no gain. I remember the Balinese telling me that the astral world is a battlefield of good versus bad and they weren't wrong there. To find love and peace, I would first have to fight myself — the demon living through me.

During my early struggles, I was literally rolling across the lounge room floor, with my mind screaming out to me for a *fucking muffin* or *chocolate!* At times, I laughed in agony at how comical this mad escapade was. I thought of the old hippy catchcry of 'love and peace' and would laugh some more to myself that hippies must have lived very sheltered lives. But over time, I learnt to sit with that pain and then, over time again, I found that the churning urge would rise for only a brief period each day, easing enough for me to hold back the negative power, followed by a great natural lift in the evenings where I would be enthusiastic about life and feeling really great. At times, after shaking, I could actually feel some fervour, emanating a beautiful flavour from my heart. Moments like these felt so much more satisfying than the illusion of drugs.

By abstaining from the craving and not getting involved in my mind's dark sideshow, I was giving myself all that I needed to build my strength. And together with my shaking practice, building more strength, 'who' I really am was beginning to see the light of day — and another, and another. For years, seeing the light of day had been walking out of a nightclub at eight in the morning.

24. Mind wide shut

OVER THE COURSE OF MANY YEARS my Western-conditioned mind had become quite sick. It had been plagued by the ancient transgressions fatal to spiritual progress — the seven deadly sins of vanity, envy, gluttony, lust, anger, greed and sloth. I had fallen into a dark abyss, terrified where it would eventually lead. Attachments to my ego, jealousy, food, being sleazy, worrying/anxiousness, partying and drugs — it had been happening to me on many levels. Many times, I could not believe the morbid, sick thoughts that popped into my head.

Mentally over-stimulated, thoughts were allowed to enter and run free, impulsively building in intensity. I remembered the Balinese telling me that the lower astral works itself through the mind. With my aura being a receiver to the spirit world, my mind was the conjunction, where the lower astral had fused a wayward filter into my world. My mind was the key to the matrix.

Subtly re-conditioned over the years, my mind had become my bogeyman. A thought would enter my mind space and be immediately energised with a body stimulation. A thought about so-and-so would make me angry, lustful, bitter or jealous; a thought about food would make me greedy; a thought about a situation would make me anxious; a thought about myself would make me sick... and on it went. Many times, the thoughts were just grim, dark visions of the world around me. 'What is driving these thoughts?' I would continually berate myself. And falling to sleep at night, I could not lay my head onto the pillow and drift off into a blissful state. I'd toss and turn for hours on end, finally turning the TV on to play a distractive trick on my mind to fall asleep — my mind finding a complementary sedative frequency to chill out. It was all energy, but it was low — negative — energy. It sapped my strength, will and clarity.

I often thought of Renee and her trauma — how strong the power of the mind was for her. Her pain was really no different from mine, with traumatised chakras and an alignment to the lower astral. I thought of other friends who had also taken their own lives. How could someone sit with a loaded gun and simply blow his head off, like my friend, Terry? And Dad, too! Their darkness had won. My world was littered with lower astral victims. And to the lower astral — victories!

I could see how out of touch society is with matters of the mind. No one — school or family — had ever taught me about the power of the mind and its ability to wreak havoc on my life, or what the signs of balance to imbalance were. More so, if I had a mind issue, it was such a taboo topic. It was okay to end up in intensive care with any type of *physical* ailment. I could unashamedly tell the world about that, but should I experience discomfort within my mind, no matter how subtle, it was a social decree that I had to keep it to myself. And to mention darkness or frequencies: 'It doesn't exist! It's all in your head you idiot!' I suppose the stigma stemmed from the old view of mental health relating to crazies running loose and throwing chairs around asylums. I was far from needing a straight jacket and didn't sit all day staring out the window, dribbling onto my shirt, nor stand at a bus stop laughing into the air, blabbering to myself; my mental discomfort was more subtle. Its voice though *was* grim. It allowed me to get on with my life and look as though I was fitting in, but it was holding me in a helpless and frightening state. It was, 'Just deal with it,' and suffer in social silence.

And as I looked around my world, I could see darkness strangling the life from this planet in many, many ways, thriving within the minds of millions, determined to conquer and destroy, rape and pillage. So why couldn't I speak of darkness in my mind when I had it pumped in my face from all over the world every night on the news? Yet, of course, the news never showed madmen, just mad acts!

One evening I turned on the television and there was a documentary about the drug 'ice' (methamphetamine) — the latest cool drug in the club scene. The location was an inner-city hospital in Sydney and a young man had been admitted to the emergency ward. He had consumed ice and to see the energetic dynamic playing out on the television screen was a spellbinding moment. This user needed four men to restrain him from his violent outbursts. Placed in a safe monitoring bay, he sat there and masturbated in view of everyone for hours on end. This was the type of dark, morbid world of the lower astral vibrational frequency I had been uncovering playing out right before my eyes, on national television. But who at home watching could explain the ultimate source of this man's Jekyll and Hyde encounter?

Two doctors assured me that my disparate mind and chronic anxiety was a biological imbalance and nothing more. The only avenue available to me in their professional opinion was medicine. Okay, my biology was imbalanced, but how does a chemical lopsidedness manifest this psycho-biological transformation and where does the change come from that turns man into monster? Mainstream society could only offer me a 'lid' to put on top of my sick, chronic thoughts and anxiety. To know exactly what was driving the thoughts and fear could not be explained to me by those medical practitioners. Medication was (and still is) the social benchmark. It was as far as we'd come — a medicinal lid! Western professors hadn't yet been able to prove anything beyond the lid.

But following authors such as Deepak Chopra, who claim the mystery of our bodies is guided by an inner intelligence that mirrors the universe, and reading books like *The Field*, I discovered that Western science continues to explore what tribal spiritualists have known for countless generations. And for science to discover the truth would be to discover the source of our existence. As the doctor was concluding his prognosis, it was truly like the scene from *The Matrix*: 'Which pill, Paul — the blue or the red?'

If I had taken that medication long term, eventually my biological body would have gotten weaker under the chemical illusion of feeling okay. But it would have been a life of further underlying pain and suffering. The conclusive crescendo of this clever game would rob me of any awareness, strength or fight. After Dad's death, I remember emptying the medicine cabinet of a plethora of prescription tablets. I asked Joyce what they all were for. There were pills for many different ailments, with quite a few needed to counteract the side effects of another one. Talk about a snowball effect. To say Dad was an alcoholic who suffered a cerebral haemorrhage certainly was only citing but a snippet of *his* astral spectrum.

To become whole, not split, another new platform needed nurturing to flourish. By shaking, being aware and meditating, silent stillness was the blissful inner void I began to find, nullifying all the negative thoughts bouncing inside my head. My list of reminders for my 'power mind at work' became an important part of my map. My list included:

- *Discipline*: working on myself; my choices; my high or low vibe.
- *Power thoughts*: positive; clear; life-loving; determined.
- *Proactive*: doing what needs to be done — now.
- *Peaceful*: at bedtime and during silence; with myself and with others.
- *Acceptance*: not judging or manipulating others; honouring the past, the path and myself.
- *Independent*: not needing the accolades of others; not giving into peer group pressure; following my heart.
- *Community*: feeling comfortable and a part of the community, and in all social situations.
- *Living in the moment*: being here, now.

But I also had to understand my 'weak mind at work'. This list included:

- *Constant cravings*: addictions and desires.
- *Destructive thoughts*: about me; people; the environment.
- *Laziness to working towards a new me*: 'I'll do it tomorrow'; 'I'll stay in bed.'
- *Sleeplessness*: mind racing at bedtime.
- *Fear*: of socialising; worthiness; confidence; success/failure.
- *Isolation*: aloneness; sharing unease; not fitting in.
- *Attachment*: to power; status; unhealthy ego; partner; partying.
- *Conditioned*: tranced out for hours with the TV or internet; influenced by fear through the media, and the mind-sets and opinions of family and friends.
- *Living away from the moment*: always thinking of yesterday or tomorrow.

25. Feeling good

SHAKING AT HOME WAS BECOMING the fundamental core of my healing. Physically and energetically, every cell within my body was being woken up by the free-flowing movement, allowing the energy on which I was focused to enter. Living in an apartment, I never got to the explosive heights like others did in Bali, but, still, I could feel myself connecting to the energy. I remembered Eric telling me in Bali how the French group trained in an apartment and one day a woman was connecting strongly to the energy and screaming out. The neighbours called the police. 'Emotional bodywork', they explained to the police, who demanded to enter the unit to see for themselves.

I could see now how healing really is an individual responsibility, and whether alone or in a group — with the right focus and attitude — the higher astral is always there to connect to. For the first time in countless years, I could feel *something* begin to open and give way. The feeling of isolation was tormenting me less, as I didn't really feel that empty yearning for old familiar experiences as strongly. My lighting job was keeping me busy — and honest — and I viewed that time as a period of change. Even the perception of being in the midst of all-consuming negativity was losing its influence. I accepted that things are as they are, and my job was to stay positive, focused and continue to make the right choices daily, and shake daily. I thought that if I could project or exude the positive work I was doing, I could influence others, not vice versa. At least by changing my perception of myself, the world may change in a small way also.

After each shaking session I continued to look at every corner of my past life, piecing together my negative acts and pursuits. I was sure there were still hidden corners I could not see, but I would see them when the time was right — when I was ready to. Strength could no longer be about muscles, an inflated ego or money; it was now about harmonising with the energy and feeling connected to myself and life. Power resides in the heart and any challenge in life could only be won with love. I thought: *Power on an ego level — nobody wins. Power on a spiritual level — everybody wins, because we become one.*

I remembered hearing in Bali that shaking without the proper focus is simply a sport. And I could see how sport could not raise one's vibration, being of a body level, whereas raising one's vibration is of a soul level. There were many stories of world-class athletes succumbing to fatal and debilitating illnesses. While exercising helped to instill a feeling of cleanliness and health, it wasn't vibrational. And I could see how I used to approach sport in the past as a dualism — through feeling good, and feeling my ego.

My sessions at the city's cool gym were once just lifting weights, hoping to look good for my Saturday night rise to the dance floor podium or the DJ box. I lived by the illusion that if I looked muscular, I must have been doing great and everyone would think: *Wow, nice bod. Who's he?* I was standing in front of the mirror — and the crowd — in an ego-induced trance, admiring the outer casing grow stiffer and harder. I was pushing weights, thinking I was looking great and getting bigger, but all that did was to give the pandemonic insides more places to hide, as my attachment to my facade blinded me internally, keeping me separate from my *overall* body.

And the mainstay of aerobic fitness for me was dancing for eight hours in a nightclub. If I was in a beautiful park and danced at the pace and duration I did on a Saturday night, then it would have been a great workout. With alcohol, drugs, smoke and stale air grinding through my system, no wonder that next morning cough sounded like a truck starting — not to mention embarrassing. And even when I was engaging in aerobic fitness, such as bike riding or swimming, I *was* trying to feel good, but subtly my ego got a workout also, as I'd ride along the 'must be seen' promenade of trendy Bondi beach, or do my swimming lap of the beach, exiting the water pumped up like a rooster pluming its feathers for all to see.

With my mind being the conjunction of the lower vibrational field, my mouth was the physical entry point for that energy to dominate. I wanted to take/eat whatever I chose. Weakened and lacking any discipline or foresight, I simply consumed with a mind-set of in-the-moment pleasure and comfort, totally disconnected to the real needs of my body. My addiction to sugar and lineage of drugs and alcohol reflected how I was not honouring my relationship with myself — via my mouth. Eating healthy, and hoping to feel good, was more than a raw food diet; it was the *energy* behind all of what I was doing and it was the *energy* behind all of how I perceived my healing to be.

Acting in a higher resonant way was monitoring my mind. I began to take notice of how I ate. My plate was swallowed before I'd take my second breath. I would watch TV, numbed out to what was *really* going into me. It was stuffed in while racing among the traffic. And in the past, I'd be worried about smelling of garlic straight after dinner, but would drench my system with alcohol and chemicals a short time later.

'Feel the energy!' At my next meal, while I was chewing my food, I had to take notice of what I was doing in my mind. Was I focused on chewing the goodness and life force that nourishment provided? Was my mouth empty before the next forkful entered? Did I sit in silence? Did I have the TV on or was I reading the newspaper? Was I thinking about this and worrying about that? Was I talking through my ego? Did I choose to sustain or salivate? Did I want to prolong the hedonistic taste till I was sickened?

The Balinese were a good example of how to eat — and act. Everything I did was fast. I talked fast, thought fast, walked fast, drove fast and ate fast. It didn't matter if the entire Balinese community were seated for a meal, there was complete silence and patience, with their eyes focused solely on the meal and nothing else. One evening I tuned into Mum's partner eating his dinner. I did admire the way he ate. I watched as he slowly cut up his serving and chewed — and chewed, and chewed — and then slowly and peacefully returned to the plate to do it again, in silence. I was ready for dessert before he had finished his entrée. My mind was intent and automated to race off to what happened yesterday or how tomorrow might turn out, and my mouth was eager to send words out instead of take food in. I had to be aware of what thoughts I was digesting and regurgitating.

'Made with 100% love,' I recalled James telling me. I compared how I felt after preparing a home cooked meal to eating take-away from the local tandoori shop. Or how I felt when I'd make my own lunch instead of eating at the dodgy hamburger restaurant. And frozen, *healthy* dinners never sat quietly on my belly. Energy was going into my food and was no more evident than how I felt *after* a take-away meal. I'd enjoy the taste of it (sometimes), but afterwards it always seemed to sit awkwardly.

It came down to good energy — or lack of it — while preparing food. Its life force had either been quashed via lifeless factory production lines or people were treating food like a simple fast-paced transaction commodity, disregarding the ancient value of food as a sacred supporter of life. Food made with love and harmony contained the optimum in energetic nutritional value. I let go of the mind trip of vitamins and minerals, or even organic. If the energy transferred into what I was eating was not good, then I was not honouring the higher vibrational field. What energetic sustenance would organic food provide if the guy preparing it at the cafe is a pothead or hated his job, or the waitress gives me one large serving of attitude? Energetically, a serving of deep fried fish and chips made with love, and served with sweetness and laughter, would be better for me.

Feeling and holding the sensation of hunger was to not act on autopilot and seek out food the moment the thought came. Overcoming my addiction to sugar saw a new attachment to food in general try to come to the fore, which was yet another reminder of the power of the energetic field intent to manipulate me. By holding for a short while, then eating food prepared in the right way, and eating it in peace, control and not overindulging, I was honouring myself. My belief in an energetic diet instead of some nutritional index on the packet of food would align me with the resonance I was working towards.

As with all of my healing, my ego needed to be kept in check. I couldn't switch my zeal for drugs onto the source of my salvation, and have a superior, self-righteous attitude. I had to be aware of the clever mind trips: thinking I am better than others because I know the right way; feeling superior to others because I eat healthier than them; being condescending to other people's lifestyles; acting cool because I shop at the organic supermarket — even becoming *fanatical* about organic or certain healing foods. All lower astral! The new journey was about honouring myself and the new energy I was working with, and humility, non-judgmental acceptance, and non-fanaticism were paramount.

An energetic diet offered me great healing inroads and no fad diet or 'bestselling bird seed' diet would be needed. Detoxifying and reconditioning my physical system — working with the power of energy — was draining me of all of the toxins that had been accumulating over the years. In the past, the morning had been the worst moment of my day. Now, I was waking earlier, my tongue was losing that furry feeling, my puffing eyes began to deflate and my back started to curve as I lifted myself from the sheets. I'd breathe in and notice that my nasal passage between the eyes was taking in full, unobstructed breaths and my lungs felt dry and hollow as they cleared. Yes, I was starting to reap the benefits of self-TLC. And knowing that my physical body was a consequence of my astral body, I began to see how I was changing overall. I had the greatest and most powerful hospital in the universe sitting within me — and the vastest library, should I learn to read its language. The key was to unravel the new boundaries in which I found myself, being aware of how I felt after every meal, after every act/experience and accepting the fact that it was now a new playing field. Eating late at night had me waking up puffy and sluggish, so I changed dinner times. The last meal of the day was normally the size of a termite's nest, so I cut it back. I didn't need any of the excess. If I felt my meal wasn't going to be prepared in the appropriate way, I'd always remember: *If in doubt — DON'T!*

I reconnected with my childhood passion of surfing. I nurtured myself in the cleansing salt water, with clean air, sunshine and nature all dousing me in goodness. I spent many weekends going to the cleanest and greenest of environments, well away from the 'look at me' scene. Surfing felt like pure high vibrational goodness. I could feel my body and energetic life force soak up that solar and aquatic massage. Other weekends, I headed for the Blue Mountains, outside of Sydney, and walked along the tracks for kilometres, sensing nature's own energetic aura fill me with positivity.

Part Four

26. Coming home

ABOUT A YEAR AFTER my trip to Bali, and working in my lighting business, I felt it was time to reconnect to the Island of the Gods. Excited at the prospect of returning to that land of the astral, I prepared myself for three weeks in Ratu's community. This time, there would be no record cases, aftershave or Versace shirts — just me and a *healthy* desire to further my quest for healing. Reflecting on the year that was, many challenges had been overcome and, at times, I had been overcome with challenges. I had unearthed many realities about myself and my world, but I knew I was still only touching the surface of my potential and strength. Still, I never knew what my body, mind and environment were going to throw at me. Tests were every-where. At times, the lure of the past lingered in my memory, often drawing upon the many exciting and sensual pleasures of partying over the years.

For years, I had surrendered my power to others to keep pace with the team and the circuit. Surrendering that power eventually presented a lonely and isolated world. This past year continued my loneliness and isolation in a way that kept the solitary prison of my past teasing me. In embarking on this wayward method of healing, I had chosen to surrender totally to myself. The new journey I was on was one, I knew, not anyone else was keen to join. 'Paul's lost it!' Actually, I was trying to find it, but I had to do it alone. I could have been another one of the crew who faded out and simply became a wild name of the past, but I wouldn't give up that easily. Gone — yes. Forgotten — maybe. Finished — no.

As I alighted from the aircraft in Bali, the equatorial air opened my pores like a preparation of sorts. I was open to travelling deeper into the astral powers that this island revered and the humid air, filled with the energy of the island, fed through me. Now, I was a bit wiser to the powers at play. Driving through the streets, the statues of Ganesha and Shiva adorning the crossroads made more sense. Heading straight for Ratu's community, I could feel the intense work of the past year finally had a chance to ignite, as I began to feel a centredness and maturity.

The drive up the mountain was again a peek into a way of life the West had long ago abandoned. Groups of elders sat and chatted with children playing nearby; an entire community were all bathing naked together in the flowing river; an old woman, bare breasted, walked along the road with a basket atop her head; people continued to smile and wave at me. It was such a respectful, innocent and unsexualised way of life. The mind sickness of the West had not invaded this corner of the world yet. I felt welcome and a sense of belonging.

As my taxi pulled into the community, curiosity drew the Balinese out to see who had arrived. Like children, they peered into the car, giggling at a newcomer's presence. I recognised familiar faces and, when they saw it was me, smiles lit up everywhere. 'Paul dari Australi!' It was like a hero's welcome. They all hugged me like I was a brother returning. It felt like I was coming home — home to a family and home to my true self. Ketut appeared and to see her face brought a huge smile to mine. The first thing she asked was if I was working in Kuta? 'No, Ketut. DJing finished forever,' I said with a smile that would not leave my face. One of the Balinese men carried my luggage and I followed him to my room. I could hear the taman was in progress and I couldn't get changed quick enough to throw myself into the training.

As soon as I walked into the taman, I was overcome with some explosive power and I began to shake with a purpose and intensity second to none. It was like the past year's effort finally had a conducive channel to let it all out and take it all in. I noticed Ratu was not present and about a dozen Westerners, whose faces I did not recognise from last time, were all shaking hard. I also noticed a young Balinese girl standing like a zombie, with a Balinese man at her side urging her to move. She had a ghostly look, a catatonic stare and was as numb as a mannequin.

At the end of the session, I laid back on the floor and drifted my mind off to the thought of truly being in paradise. I could feel the energy flowing through me and realised how intense the past year had been. I was back now and I knew that, with the support of Ratu, the other shakers and the Balinese, the pain and commitment of the past year was worth every bit of it, and I could feel it was time to go deeper and heal more of the past.

Attending dinner, the group introduced themselves to me and their friendliness was easy to connect to. I still felt a bit tense sitting close with everyone, as the anxiety of the past lingered. But compared to a year ago, it was manageable and I acknowledged to myself its easing. Excited and wide eyed at being back in Bali, I sat after dinner and with a cup of tea began chatting to a woman who had introduced herself earlier as Tamara, from Italy. She had the typical southern Italian look. She was dark and mysterious and her English was good, having lived in London for the past eight years — even though her reverse placement of a few words here and there was cute. I couldn't help but correct her 'Where it is?' with a cheeky grin. We found a nice chemistry, but I felt that she could sense I was protective and a bit shut off and we kept the conversation on the surface, but it felt good to connect to someone on the same path.

With a room to myself this time, I woke up the following morning at 6 a.m. with no alarm to kick start my day. I went to the taman for the morning shake. Ratu was already chatting and laughing with the Balinese. I remembered from my last visit that Ratu and the Balinese were always laughing when chatting, and their humour (even though I couldn't understand it) would always bring a smile to my face. When he saw me he called out my name and walked towards me and, with arms outstretched, gave me another one of his incredible hugs, also asking, 'You work in discotheque?'

'No, Ratu, here for shaking only.'

'Very good, now you shake,' then in an instant directing me to begin the session. I could feel his warmth, love, concern and humour, but also his discipline.

That morning after breakfast I noticed the Balinese preparing for what looked like an important ceremony. Tall stilts of bamboo were decorated with small offerings wilting off the trunks, and placed along the street. Statues and temples were draped with chequered cloths and all of the Balinese seemed to be occupied in some way with the ceremony. I admired the Balinese devotion to the spiritual world. All day, every day of the year, offerings are patiently prepared by the women and ceremonial structures prepared by the men. Temples large and small cover the island. The smaller temples are the size of post boxes, and are placed on roads and rice fields, and in houses, cars and offices. And today the entire community — as part of the island collectively — were all enthusiastically doing their bit.

I asked what all the preparation was for and was informed that in a few days it would be Bali's Lunar New Year—Nyepi. A sacred day, Nyepi is embraced as a day of silence, fasting and meditation, with no electricity, no working, no entertainment, no travelling on roads or use of the airport, no eating and no sleeping from 6 a.m. till 6 a.m. the following day. The entire island literally shuts down. With the community preparing for the arrival of their revered day, I was told that it would be powerful for me to fast with them — no water and no food. Sleep could be optional for me.

I was getting to know the other Westerners during mealtimes and between the sessions. They were from Belgium, Italy, Spain, the US, France, Japan, Ireland and the UK. Young, middle-aged and elderly, everyone was friendly and committed to working with the healing powers of the astral world. But I could tell that collectively everyone knew that this journey was one that required staunch focus and determination. Seeing these Western people working with the power of astral energy was reassuring, making this journey seem less of a lonely path to tread. I really was with like-minded now and that felt good.

After a few good sessions in the taman, I could once again feel myself building up to a great energetic space during the day and evening. Once I broke through the mental blocks at the start of each session, I experienced clarity of mind, lightness in the body and a connectedness to myself and the community. It was like these were the fruits of my labour for the past year's hard work, trusting the astral world and acknowledging the power of working *with* energy.

The evening prior to the fast, I ate quite liberally, fearfully abandoning my new approach to food and eating. I was concerned that I would not have the sustenance to get through the next thirty-plus hours. 'No problem, connect to the energy and it will feed you,' said one of the Balinese. Still, a fearful voice inside my head convinced me that I would need a full stomach to get through. That evening laying in bed, feeling awkwardly full, it dawned on me that one belief that is common to the major religions is fasting.

On the morning of Nyepi, the stillness in an already-still surroundings was bliss. I could sense that nothing was happening at all over the island. It was an incredible feeling of serenity. Apart from the lighting of a fire offering, which I was told would avert the rain, the Balinese sat in reflection and it was time out from the religious rite of staying active. But then everyone entered into the taman and began shaking. It seemed as though, on this auspicious day, we had an omnipotent way of honouring the astral Gods. Even for the Balinese, the shaking practice held precedence, as their training *was* devoting themselves to the powers of the highest realm of the astral world. I was still concerned I may not make it through the day —

especially shaking — and I could feel myself holding back during the morning session, still fearful of not having energetic sustenance.

After what would have been breakfast, Tamara strolled by my room and I asked if she would like to sit and chat. We sat on my bed and she asked, 'Is this the first fast you have done, Paul?'

'Yes, I'm not sure if I will get through it, but I'm loving the atmosphere here at the moment.'

'We couldn't pick a better time or place to do a fast. You can really feel a sense of support here and across the island. When I arrived I did quite a few fasts and they have been very powerful in helping me to break through physical and emotional barriers and move me closer to the energy. It's really shown me where my desires and attachments are and also given me more clarity to see where the enemy is inside of me.'

After about ten minutes of comfortable chatting, Tamara inquired, 'Paul, are you feeling okay?'

'Well, I've been partying and taking drugs for twenty years and it did make me quite sick, in the body and the mind.'

'I've never taken drugs in my life, but I know how destructive they are. So many people around the world are suffering because of them.'

'Too many!' I went on to say how I had been shaking for the past year on my own after my initial visit here and it had helped me greatly, but I could feel that I still needed a lot more work. I asked if she knew James from England and she said that he was one of the guys who helped her in London. We talked about the incredible information I had received and how so many things now are much clearer. I then returned the same question to Tamara, more from curiosity than anything else.

'About four or five years ago I was diagnosed with endometriosis. My right ovary was not functioning and the left one was impaired. The doctor placed a camera and some instrument inside of me hoping to burn the cysts, but he found there were too many to burn and some had entered my urethra. The doctor told me that I would need medication for life. I did a medication treatment for one year, but I was always feeling depressed, and so I stopped taking the medication.

'After about three years, I could feel a big bump in my belly and I was in pain night and day. I went to see a gynaecologist and was told a big cyst, possibly a tumour, had formed. It was nine-by-six centimetres and, with the endometriosis going unchecked for so long, there was a big chance the tumour was malignant. The doctor wanted to operate quickly because the surrounding organs weren't functioning properly, and I said yes. I was living in London at the time and I had already begun the shaking practice, but I was not fully open and dedicated to the potential of the energy. But then, something clicked and I decided to try and work with energy to heal myself — with serious conviction. I became convinced that I could do it.'

'Wow, pretty full-on,' I said. 'So what happened?'

'Something urged me to cancel the operation and my doctor said, quite assertively, I would become infertile and serious other consequences were probable if I didn't undergo surgery — quick. My family were furious at my decision, but I left my job, rented out my apartment and next thing you know I'm here in Bali. I've been here for the past five months training every day.'

'How is it now?'

'Well, it's been quite challenging, but the swelling has gone down and the pain is less now. I can feel that it's under control.'

'That's incredible; it has all changed from shaking?'

'And from understanding the dynamics of energy. I've had to understand how this sickness was being fed and I've found a new lease on life by taking back control of my own. My family are worried and think I'm irresponsible. Even now when I talk to my mother and tell her I'm well and the cyst is going down, she doesn't want to acknowledge it. She keeps telling me to get back to Italy or England and go see the doctor. Italian mammas can be quite stern with their kids, so it has been challenging in that regard too.'

I felt totally inspired by Tamara's story. Another example of the power of the energetic vibrational field had my resolve strengthen even more so. I thought of how invasive the lower astral is in our world today. Drugs, tumours and sickness in general — it seemed that life today is sickness and suffering worldwide. You may live drug-free, but here you go — take this tumour. You may think you have a wonderful family, but here you go — cancer will change your bliss. You may think you are about to enjoy retirement with your loved one, but here you go — take this stroke to keep you both suffering.

As I looked into Tamara's deep, brown eyes, she smiled with a caring warmth, and tentatively asked, 'Paul, do you have a problem being close to people? I hope I'm not being too nosey.'

'No, I don't mind you asking at all. I have a problem being too close to people physically *and* emotionally. To be honest, most times I would rather shut myself away from anything that moves, and hide. I loved the warmth and connectedness when I first started taking ecstasy, but eventually it turned me cold and disconnected. I became Ice Man. Although the past year has seen that ease, I do have a bit of work to do. There's still more to melt. It was tough doing it — healing — alone in Sydney, but I was getting better. There were so many influences and challenges, especially alone in a big city, but here, around other shakers, I'm confident I can break through even stronger.'

'That's why I asked if you were okay. I could sense at the dinner table you were a bit tense, beyond shyness, and also when we chatted the other night. I'd like to help you if I may.'

'I would love you to help me.'

'When the time is right, I will.'

We realised that the morning had flown and it was time to enter the taman. I thanked Tamara for her sweetness — and also for keeping my mind from the thought of food all morning. I still held back during the shaking session, noticing this fear of not being able to get through the day on empty. But others around me were really going for it and Ratu was working everyone up into another one of his trademark frenzies. I could have given better, but I didn't.

The afternoon was a long yearning for food and I could feel a headache grind away. I was really struggling and wasn't sure if I could get through the rest of the day without eating. Joan, an elderly lady from Ireland, was supportive, saying in a thick Irish accent, 'Tonight when you train, push as hard as you can. If you can connect strongly to the energy, the energy will connect to you — it will feed you.'

I knew she was right and her pep talk softened the mental antagonism for food and sustenance. Plus, I found there was something motivating about an Irish accent.

In the last session of the day, under the soft candescence of candlelight, I decided to go for it. With no food or water all day, the shaking session leapt to another level. Before entering the taman, I was craving anything my taste buds would acknowledge and it was quite tough but, on commencing the session, I clicked into mode and felt a surge in power I had never known existed within me. With lightness in my body and mind, it felt like there was absolutely no resistance in me and I again hit *that* space where I was on a mystical horse being carried upwards. After the session I was alert, chatty and simply wanted to engage everyone. The desire for food had left and I could actually feel my body vibrating — *physically*. My senses sharpened and my perception of life rose to a beautiful new height. *Yet another link of the lower vibrational chain being broken, with this ancient religious deity of fasting and shaking,* I thought.

That evening I couldn't get to sleep. It was not like the drug-induced insomnia of the past. I felt alive and wanted to go and find anyone to chat to. I never knew I could feel so amazing without drugs — this was the real thing. But then the thought came: *Is this state an attachment? I have an addictive history and how will I know if I'm attached or desiring this state?* I immediately overrode the thought. Feeling alive, naturally, could not possibly be an attachment if I was working *with* the energy and I wasn't doing it through my negative ego. Anyway, to get to this state, enter into it and hold on to it, I had to work hard in a way that shattered the hard negative shell I'd built around me. The lower astral was easy to enter. Laziness and desires go hand in hand, but to exude wholeness and buzz with life, a dedication to working with the energy and feeling its beautiful power needed to be a whole-hearted effort and commitment. Living *is* loving life and honouring the work that complements that need. I could feel I wanted to connect from some warmth filling my heart.

A couple of days after the fast, I woke up one morning with a process, unlike any of the others. Feeling sick all over, not only was my body feeling wiped out, but also my mind seemed to open some anxious floodgate from the past. I could feel the urge for sugar biting away again. It was strong and I was bedridden for a couple of days, with neither the physical nor the emotional strength to move or engage anyone. The Balinese, as always, were as sweet as only the Balinese can be, bringing me the standard convalescent dish, bubur (mashed-up rice and vegetables), and massaging my head with a hot menthol-type of oil.

Tamara passed by my room often and her presence was comforting and supportive. Her being near me felt less lonely, as this process brought up the feeling of a sick and abandoned little boy. She was telling me how good this process is, and that combined with the fast, I had been training strong since I arrived and it had shifted some deep blocks. I thanked the energy for this gift of release. After the process passed, it was like I had to build momentum up again with shaking, as well as my overall physical and emotional strength.

I admired Joan for following this path. I held a stereotypical vision of elderly women as either being staunch church goers and 'that's as far as spirituality goes', or the 'meat and three vegies' brigade, oblivious to anything holistic, organic or heartfelt. With a conviction in her words, she said at the dinner table, 'When you process like you just did, Paul, the energy can seem like it flattens you. But with its passing, you enter a new level of resonance. You are breaking through your hardened negative conditioning. When you break through that, with all that you are now doing with the energy, your processes will not sink you to the depths of your previous one — if you continue to stay on track with the energy. Slowly, you'll spiral upwards, discarding the old layers via processing, but less severely. The early processes are tough, Paul, but you've been working with the energy for a year now and, when you returned here and lifted your intensity with the training up a level, you *had* to process. I know you've heard this before, but it really is great that you are processing strong. You *are* breaking through.'

That's one of the things I loved about following this new path — everyone understood the importance of processing and was always supporting others who were struggling. There was no judgment, disgust or procrastination. We all understood the importance of this path, and that what is inside, creating havoc, is not the real person, but simply an energetic force manifesting negatively.

About half way through an afternoon session, the Balinese men dragged what looked like a madman into the taman. We all stopped shaking and cautiously stood back. The man, Balinese, was totally berserk. He was lashing out at those trying to subdue him, spitting at them and screaming something inaudible. He looked possessed. About six men held him down, slapping his face into compliance and then tying him up. He was totally gone. One of the Balinese forced tobacco juice into his mouth. After a brief period he calmed down. I asked one of the Balinese what the problem was. 'Bad spirit taken over body, him safe here!'

I thought, *He's safe but who's going to protect us from him?*

I had known from my trips to Bali about the power of magic, especially black magic, which was often a debilitating way to exact revenge upon someone with a curse. Not only in Bali but also the islands all over Indonesia still perform these lower astral rituals. Many villages had powerful mystics who held the power of these ancient secrets and perform such acts. Many times the victims are young, beautiful girls who reject a marriage proposal, or a bright and career-oriented person who has ignited jealousy from a family member. They are powerful, incapacitating and highly acknowledged acts of the astral still called upon — and another sign for me of its reality in this life. This man's father had brought him to the community to shake in the hope of its passing, and for his own, and others', safety.

As the days passed, the darker shadows of myself were gaining more clarity for me to see and feel. I knew there were many subtle influences working their own splintered matrixes within me still, most of which I habitually and automatically connected to daily. I'd overcome many challenges over the past year and I had to acknowledge huge victories over daily sugar binges, the abandonment of the spiralling club scene, drugs, and a change in my health for the better. Those were major battles hard-won. I had weakened, if not severed many channels. Yet I could still see many more that were pushing buttons inside of me that just appeared at given moments, such as anger, frustration, lingering morbid thoughts, attachments to old thought patterns and material things, and lingering anxiety. Many inner traumas as far back as my childhood, buried deep, would need to be shaken free and I wasn't sure how long that would take, but acknowledging changes in my state so far instilled trust that time would sort things out.

One afternoon I saw Ratu seated on his own. Without a thought, I approached him. He smiled and asked me to sit. Folding his legs in lotus position and looking at me quite attentively, it was as though he was waiting for me to speak, rather than initiating conversation himself.

'Ratu, I feel I understand more about myself, my sickness and the energy now,' I said, not really putting any thought into what I was trying to convey.

'Very good. You sensitive and that good for feeling energy. You have sweet heart but must not connect to mind. Mind want to keep you down. You must be free. You keep shaking and you will be stronger.'

After a long pause, Ratu stared above my head, and I wasn't sure whether to say something else or get up and leave. Then Ratu continued, 'Very important you heal yourself. Then you can share your experience with others. When you heal, then you understand energy. Then you help people. You have teacher inside. Ratu no teacher. Me is you, you is me — we are all one.'

I had heard it on my previous visit, but now it made more sense why Ratu had never given us any theory or instructions. We *do have to* find the answers ourselves. Since I've worked with it, I feel it resonating. Now I'm feeling it, I'm understanding it — I'm understanding me. It seems his role is to help people connect to themselves, and for those committed to understanding life and themselves, the answers will appear. I had to experience *experience* to become aware of it.

With a smile on my face, I said that I had been very frustrated with him during my initial visit, and that I felt he wasn't telling me many things, but now I understand more from feeling the energy. Ratu, finding some humour in my comment, said, 'Energy like car. If I give you book to read on car, you very clever and understand book very well. But when you drive car for first time, what you read about driving car very different to driving car. To understand energy, you must feeling. Only feeling, can you understand energy. If people no want to understand energy now, one day they understand.' Ratu smiled at me again, placed his hand on my head and concluded our conversation with a gesture to move on. I thanked him and felt lifted by our brief but purposeful chat.

During both my stays, Ratu seemed to leave us to be responsible for ourselves, as though we were all in control of and guiding our own destiny. There was motivation in the taman from Ratu, and he used many 'tools' to motivate us during the shaking sessions. Sometimes, with a hand on some part of our body, he would work our intensity up. At times, he would walk among us, giving out handfuls of rice or chillies, which would send the taman into fiery bedlam. Chewing on chillies the size of AAA batteries certainly got us all feeling inside. I learnt later that Ratu instills an energetic blessing on what he hands out to us — sometimes chillies, rice, a biscuit, or even a flower.

To the unsuspecting, the taman in full flight would look like a madhouse, but that madness is the burning of the lower astral energy. And, in doing so, all the answers appear for us. And just as Ratu said to me, 'Important to share my experiences,' that is what others had done for me. They had shared their experiences of energy, helping me along so I may understand myself, my ways and my way. I remembered a year back when I felt Ratu was showing a total disregard for me and I then recalled an old saying: only a wise man can play the fool. Ratu's words to me, although brief and in broken English, were heart to heart.

As I walked back to my room I passed an elderly man who was seated near the taman. I said, 'Hi,' and introduced myself. His name was Christos, from Spain, and he asked how I was doing. I hadn't seen him at the dinner table at all, only shaking in the taman.

I said, 'Fine,' pointing to the seat next to him, indicating if it were okay to sit and have a chat.

'Please do,' he said, as he ran his fingers through his greyish beard.

'I haven't seen you around much outside of the taman,' I inquired.

'I've been fasting since I arrived.'

'When did you arrive?'

'Thirty-two days ago.'

'Wow, that's incredible. Just water?'

'A rice fast.'

'Rice fast?'

'Rice is a sacred grain, and if prepared in the right way; it's energetically pure and a powerful fast.'

'Well, I must say, you look fantastic.'

'Thanks, Paul. Shaking has been feeding me energy also. Fasting and shaking together is very powerful.'

We chatted about where we both were from and what we did. Christos had a yoga practice in Spain. He'd been teaching yoga for almost twenty years.'

'Have you found this practice helps yours?' I asked.

'Most certainly. My classes have many people attending. Working with the awareness I've gained from shaking has helped me see how much I wasn't teaching from a clean space. I subtly held my students under me, always projecting that they can achieve but not overtake me. It was very difficult to accept when I began to see it inside of me. It has been a huge test for me because the more I discovered this negativity, and the more I worked on healing it, the more I could see it trying to influence me during my classes. Having students looking up to me, with many putting me on a pedestal, has been a powerful channel for my weakness — my ego. Plus, there was a time when the shaking practice was only for me. It was my Bali secret. But now I offer all of my students the shaking practice, and we now have regular shaking nights. By surrendering to my fear of losing my students to pursue only shaking, more and more newcomers keep turning up to my yoga classes and our shaking nights continue to grow. It's been an amazing learning opportunity.'

I listened to Christos with an appreciation of his honesty. Once he finished, he asked how I was finding the practice, and I shared with him my journey.

With a concerned look he said, 'My son and all his friends are into the rave scene and I know they are taking a lot of drugs. I've tried to help him change course, but he thinks he's invincible at the moment... kids! One day, he'll need to understand it all. We all do eventually.'

'I'm hoping this is my one and only wake-up call.'

'Once you move forward, Paul, new tests will come in life and you must — we all must — be prepared for those. Processes change as your vibration ascends and the astral will continue to test you. These may not necessarily be physical blocks, but more life-oriented. Look at me. I've lived a spiritual life for over twenty years and the energy is giving me a huge test with the way *I'm* living. I'm working with a vibrational practice — and remember vibrational energy means intelligence beyond our minds. As the coordinator, I have a powerful influence over everyone in my class. If I am not clear — energetically — then the class really is under me and my stuff, and no one will get the chance to truly harmonise with a higher vibration.'

With a curiosity as eager as my fist day at the ashram, I asked, 'It's surprising that a vibrational practice such as yoga didn't open your awareness to your negative side. It took shaking to bring it to your senses?'

'Yes, it wasn't until I began shaking that things suddenly appeared for me to become aware of. You see, shaking really cuts to the chase, as I think you say in English. The way the world is today, many vibrational techniques are too passive. One-thousand years ago things may have been different, but today to raise one's vibration in a stagnated world requires an active approach. And if you can raise your vibration, then process occurs — the negative *has* to come out. Yoga instills more of a body awareness, whereas shaking offers those who can connect to the energy a way to clear deep energetic — astral — blocks and move deeper, on a soul level, unless you are a life-long yogic.

'Teaching yoga is my livelihood and powerful if performed — and facilitated — energetically correct. Now I can instill a cleaner environment during classes. My understanding of energy doesn't undermine the potential of my classes, so far as creating a space where yoga's gifts may be experienced. My role now is to ensure that while we are doing our asanas, the energy is focused and tuned into a higher resonant mind-set. I'm happy with both my yoga classes being performed in a powerful space, and the shaking group, which allows us all to work in a more rigorous way, and focus on the energetic channel Ratu has offered us.'

'Do you find much resistance from newcomers to the group when shaking?'

'Yes, for some shaking can be too intense, as it can bring up a lot of emotional blocks and stir many things up. The pain may be too great, or the incredible power of working with energy in that way may become overwhelming. But this is the test each individual faces. Living is karma and karma is process. Shaking is such an incredible way to release, heal and understand life. Some people in my yoga classes just want a passive approach to feeling good, without going too deep, and that is their journey. If I can facilitate a powerful space for them, then they are able to get the best possible help from me as a yoga teacher. Shaking moves *everything* and allows me greater introspection. Shaking is beyond a practice; it's a way to feel and become aware and sensitive to life, which is energy. We reconnect to the universal web of energy.'

Seeing people entering into the taman, it was time to reconnect to the energy and myself. Thanking Christos, we both rose from our chairs and made our way to the taman. With an affirmative nod to Christos, we separated and I found myself a space and began to shake, initially letting my mind remain intrigued by the incredible people I was meeting.

Between sessions, the ashram felt truly like a peaceful haven. The women, as always, were seated together preparing offerings, chatting, and always calling out my name when I passed by. It was like life was not about rushing, and the Balinese capitulated that state of being in the moment, and harmonious, no matter what the task at hand.

One afternoon I saw a group of Balinese fussing over a newspaper article. The media was warning the public about a person or group of people from some part of the country who were sending mobile phone text messages, testing their black magic skills via the telephone. Already a number of people had become ill, even hospitalised from opening the messages from a specific number, which were cast with lower astral spells. Here was one of the country's leading newspapers warning the public about such matters. The Balinese, reading the piece, took it seriously. I thought if a newspaper ran a story like that in Sydney, it could only be April Fool's Day. The astral world was showing me continually in this land how relevant it is. The lower realms of the astral continued to appear for me to see their manifestations, as I worked away at becoming more sensitive.

Outside of shaking, Tamara and I found ourselves chatting long after mealtimes. I found her company very soothing, and I was spending most of my free time with her. I wondered if there was any connection beyond friendship, but I had become too conditioned to some instant desirous explosion towards women during the past. That explosion hadn't happened with her, though I found myself always sitting next to her at the dinner table, chatting about life or whatever. She possessed some emotional strength that I found was centred with a deep power that radiated in her eyes. I found this strength very attractive and being in her presence was relaxing and nurturing. It was that type of strength I needed. I was amazed after telling her all about my seedy past that she didn't react with disgust or judgment, telling me that it was not who I really am, that all of that history is simply a negative energy that needed cleansing.

I had been inquisitively following the progress of the two

Balinese who had black magic cast on them. The man had regained most of his senses, and I could see he was more in his body now. His stare was still vacant, but he was totally different from the person who had been dragged into the ashram a couple of weeks earlier. There was life back in his entire body. The woman was still dazed, with a somewhat staggered gait, but she was coherent now and aware of herself and others around her. She now looked like such a sweet and innocent girl, with that ghastly look now drained from her. They both were shaking without any coercing and their faces were more relaxed, losing that vacant facade that had startled me earlier. *The power of the astral,* I again thought to myself.

One evening as the session was ending, Ratu asked us all to cease training and sit in the taman. After a few minutes for everyone to regain some composure, Ratu's greeting of 'Om Swastiastu' was returned, and with the help of Wayan translating, Ratu began to talk.

'If people understand themselves, then life is simple and life is beautiful. But if they don't understand themselves, they don't want to live. Now people can heal themselves, to uncover the potential inside as is written in *The Vedas*. This transcendental healing is inside each and every one. Each and every sickness can be healed within. We have the medicine inside. Shaking sends electricity to all of our cells and atoms, waking them up. This electricity is like a disinfectant for the blood and we stay healthy.

'You must change the patterns of the mind, the way of thinking, so that your life becomes full of happiness, a sense of safety, full of peace and prosperity, and feel grateful and find the potential inside you until you can laugh. The power of the divine wakes up and guides you, so that you are free of sickness and free of the difficulties of life and free of everything. For this, let us work hard and pray as much as we can. The full potential wakes up and guides us to become our true selves. If we are our true selves, we don't have any difficulties in our lives. Life becomes

26. Coming home

beautiful and loving towards each other. We all have the power of leader, but it is asleep.'

After a long silence, Ratu thanked us all, gave us another one of his warm smiles and left the taman.

I could finally begin to gain a sense of the mystery of Ratu. He was a simple man, but he was knowledgeable on a level that most are not. He had an innate understanding of the complexities of people and the astral world. What science claims as mystery, Ratu follows as universal wisdom, sharing it with others so they may better their lives. Through our free will, we can connect to the energetic channel he lives his life for. This channel he works with is within all of us, but not active. He doesn't promise that he can heal us; he only claims that he can help us to reactivate that healing energy of the sacred fire within us. It is we who must work hard, and also believe that we do have that energy inside of us, which can be accessed and used for our growth, health and happiness.

* * *

It was nearing the end of my stay and with the three intense shaking sessions daily, I felt physically exhausted, but grounded and with a fire in the eyes. I could see my face had changed remarkably. It was relaxed, clear and more open. Even the colour of my eyes had become stronger. I was feeling for the first time in countless years that I could sit with a group of people and engage them in a mature and relaxed conversation. The past *was* melting away and my life was being reclaimed. I was breaking free of the lower vibrational field, and living — not simply existing.

It just so happened that a week or so after I was to return to Australia, Tamara's visa expired and she had to leave the country. She had planned to either go to Singapore for a visa run and return, or head back to England. But with no job to return to and her apartment tenanted, she was unsure of the best option. She felt she had her tumour under control, but would need to keep training strong.

'Why don't you come to Australia?' I curiously asked.

'That thought did cross my mind. I have the feeling you may need some support there, being all on your own, and staying connected to the energy may be challenging for you. Together we can train strong and support each other.'

'Is this the help you were offering me?'

'Could be.'

On my last night, I entered the taman late in the evening and laid down on the floor, facing skywards. I thought about my long journey up to that moment. Discovering my heart's yearning for fulfilment, I also realised this entire journey of healing — the anxiety, the physical pain and emotional torment — were all guides to finding myself. Like Dad's death, and the experience of my belongings being stolen in Amsterdam many years before, nothing is good or bad, it just is. I thought, *What if I did lead a 'normal' life of being the family man next door, with a nice job and coach of the local football side? I may never have discovered all that I had.* My life, in all of its negativity, led me — step by rickety step — to the discovery of the real me.

It was my pain that synchronised many encounters, showing me the way. It was my pain that offered me experiences that would help me understand life better. It was my pain that led me to discovering my own truth. And peering through the pain, I began to feel a sense of forgiveness. Forgiving Mum and Dad for fighting — they *were* decent people and gave us kids the best they possibly could. Forgiving Mum for leaving us — I knew she carried as much pain as I did for all that had happened. And forgiving myself. If I could discover the true essence of my heart, then all of the trauma I suffered, and all of the pain Mum and Dad endured themselves, was one of the most powerful offerings imaginable. An offering that, through their struggle, their son found peace in the world.

The moment arrived to bid farewell to my friends, though this time it did feel as though my adieu was not farewell. The community of Ratu Bagus was now like a new family and my parting company was to carry the strength of their love and support back home. I felt like I would never be alone now in my quest for seeking peace and happiness, with new friends here in Bali and across the world, all working with the love of the universe. The past three weeks offered me a priceless opportunity to go deeper into myself and understand the complexities of life to an even greater degree. With my past distancing itself further from my life and the lingering pain that had tormented me for so long easing even further, I felt for the first time that total healing and ongoing health were a certainty should I continue on with this vocation.

As the circle formed, with everyone singing me goodbye, I came to Tamara. We hugged. As we embraced, I could feel the warmth of our hearts enmesh and, both not wanting to separate, we held that kindling fuzziness. I had never felt a physical connection like it from anyone ever before.

'I will see you in Sydney in a week,' she said, as we eased ourselves apart.

'Let me know your arrival details and I will pick you up from the airport. Thank you so much for all your support. It has been a beautiful experience meeting and spending time with you.' We looked into each other's eyes and smiled.

'See you soon,' I said.

Ratu was there at the completion of the circle and his face emanated a look of joy. With his arms reaching out, he wrapped them around me and hugged me like I was a son leaving home to brave the world. I thanked him for everything, as a few teardrops cascaded down my smiling face. Saying goodbye never felt so beautiful.

27. Coming together

TAMARA'S ARRIVAL IN AUSTRALIA had me feeling more excited than I had felt in a long time. That first afternoon, she asked if she could cook me dinner, and we went to the local delicatessen to buy some Italian groceries. That evening, I experienced a feeling that I had long ago abandoned — the smell of a home cooked meal being prepared for me in my own home. I sat like a little boy on the sofa as she cooked in the kitchen, feeling so comforted, and a peaceful energy filled my house. Dinner was served, and I took my first bite of some amazing dish she had prepared. My eyes began to swell, and I found it difficult to hold back the emotion. I placed my fork back to the plate and stared into her eyes, as a teardrop fell from my star struck eyes.

'Nobody has ever done this for me before. Not for a very long time. It sounds crazy, but this meal is the most beautiful experience I have ever had. I can feel so much caring and sweetness from you. Thank you.'

'This is my pleasure, Paul,' her smile radiating the care I was feeling from her.

With a smile I said, 'What did you put into this food?'

'My Nonna, sorry, Grandmother, taught me to prepare food like you are caring for a baby. It's that important.'

'If you can care for a baby the way you cook, you'll make an incredible mother.' She laughed.

I continued to eat, and each bite was like it was filling a deep hole that had remained empty since I was fourteen years old. It stirred up memories of when Mum left us and what a dreadful period of my life that was. Her cooking for us kids every night, and then suddenly it disappearing, was something I always missed. Tasting Tamara's cooking made me realise how much love Mum put into *her* food for us. She did love us all very much.

After dinner Tamara went to the kitchen and returned with a

plate of some Italian dessert. I became scared. *Sugar,* I thought.

Tamara looked at me and said, 'Paul, if you eat with the right energy and respect, you'll be fine.'

We shared the dessert and it was the first time I had eaten sugar with respect for a very long time.

Our connection continued to deepen romantically, and without any anticipation for the future, each day felt more and more natural being with Tamara. Our intimate moments were like I was learning to love and express affection for the very first time. I had been with many women over the years, and never once did I ever touch on the virtue of intimacy. Renee was close, but that experience was just a passing experience because of her tragedy. Tamara helped me to see further shadows which needed attention, and her patience, understanding and care offered me a safe environment to expose my vulnerabilities and heal more of the past. Because of her sweetness, and strength, I began to learn how to express love to another person, and to myself.

Tamara planned to stay for three months, and she kept me company as I drove around the city installing lights. We never found it difficult to chat about any topic, and when there was nothing to say, it was very peaceful. One day she said that it would be good if I kept a journal and wrote down my experiences as a way of piecing together my journey. I thought it was a good idea, and so I went to a newsagent and bought an exercise book, which was to be my journal. When I opened the book at home, a lottery ticket fell from the covers. Someone had marked out their chosen numbers, but had not entered the ticket at the cash register. I thought it may be a good omen, and so, the following day, I took the ticket back to the newsagent and entered it.

A week later, we sat excitedly in front of the TV and watched the coloured balls drop.

'We have that number. We have that number also. And that one...' We had six numbers out of seven. We couldn't believe it, thinking like kids all sorts of incredible figures we may have won. The next day we got a nice surprise: $3,000 — and a message to keep writing.

We continued training together and supporting each other on our new path — the path of the higher vibrational field. Tamara continued to help me to see hidden corners of myself that I still could not. And as I gained a further understanding of energy, I began to help her heal the deep wounds that manifested her sickness. There was never anything but sweetness in her words of advice and encouragement. The more I shared with her my complex past and my dark secrets, the simpler my relationship became with her, allowing me to feel secure and worthy. Her caring sweetness helped Ice Man melt away. I laid myself bare with no shame and no bravado. And what I received was such a caring woman, who continued to see through the energy of the past, to a man who was searching for his heart.

As fate would have it, she decided to spend more time with me in Australia and our relationship developed in a way I never anticipated. Two years from the time we first met, we married. Deciding to see where our mixed cultural union would flourish best, eventually we decided Bali would be a good compromise, and also allow us to be nearer the path we had both chosen to follow. And so a new chapter of my life began, but now I was not alone.

Both our lives had changed for the better since embarking upon the path of shaking and working with the higher vibrational field. Yet we were uncertain if Tamara had fully healed herself from the tumour that was to render her sterile — and possibly cost her her life if not treated or removed surgically. One day we received a precious gift from the universe... a son.

Final Note

28. Wanna get high?

WELL, THIS IS THE PART OF the journey where, like most down-and-out stories, I'm expected to share with you the incredible new life I now live and my rewards for taking up the fight for a gallant cause. But to outright finish like that is not what I am trying to accomplish in writing this book. This book was not initiated to sing high praises about what *I* achieved. It was spawned by a deep desire to help others better understand themselves and our world. By sharing all I have experienced and learnt, my hope is it may instill a new belief of hope, healing and happiness within you.

I was blessed with two opportunities, which allowed the blindfold to be removed from my senses, showing me how the world really does spin. Drugs set the stage; my healing showed me the entire ensemble. Drugs took me to the very edge, preparing me for either death or transformation. Strangely, if I had never embarked on my Sex, Drugs and Techno lifestyle, the understanding of energy and darkness would have seemed somewhat less relevant and tangible. It is like it was meant to be. Experiencing and then understanding the astral energetic vibrational field that I lived, worked and played with during my wild days was to embrace that celestial field and work *with* its positive influence as a way to heal.

This book has been about the reality of drugs, which ultimately uncovers the reality of the lives that people are living. There is an entire generation out there trashing themselves and their lives every week, with no way of knowing how to pull themselves back when reality sets in. Outside of the cool inner-city scene, there are shanty towns littered across the world where people live in squalid conditions, reliant on drugs to get through each day. These places are beyond Third World. Drugs are a global plague, destroying lives with greater force than war.

Why me? As I have shared throughout this book, I have lost many friends — too many. I feel a strong calling to help the countless numbers of — mostly — young people who are suffering around the world from the destructive force of drugs and other harmful attachments. Too many never had a second chance and too many are resigned to the realisation that health and happiness are simply a memory of days gone by. I hope that my second chance allows others the same opportunity. I am not special. I simply refused to give in to where my lifestyle was ultimately leading me.

I once viewed spirituality as a topic only the weak would follow. As I have learnt, embracing the higher astral world is far from being weak — quite the contrary. The reason there is so much destruction and disregard for life on this planet is because of humans' total abandonment of universal spiritual harmony. To destroy all things, and follow a gluttonous mind — that is weak. To embrace wholeness, pure potentiality and union — that requires an incredible amount of courage.

My vibrational healing journey has acquainted me with the most primitive people through to the most prominent holistic therapists and practitioners in the West. From drug users, to trades people, to housewives, to bankers — all walks of life, all seeking the transformational powers of working with vibrational energy. The greatest revelation for me is that people, regardless of race, culture or societal/holistic attitudes, are influenced by the lower vibrational field permeating our world today. For some, this hidden force plays through the personality; for others, it is vastly more serious. Our world and its inhabitants are in desperate need of transformation. We are all energetic magnets and our world has become tainted. We suffer if we do not keep our energetic homes clean.

The more I healed via working with astral energy, the more I discovered further layers of myself not in harmony with how my new perception was ascending. *Still today*, there are personality traits that I wish to/need to work at harmonising. It is the many, ongoing complexities of being human in today's world that makes embracing the higher vibrational field a lifelong commitment. Only time and a commitment to the higher vibrational field can unearth the obscure shadows within us, which others may see and sense.

To write now that every single day of my life is like a scene from a movie of glory, standing at the top of a mountain peak, would not be right, and I'm always sceptical of endings like that. I accept that some days I am more enthusiastic than others. Some days I need to push a bit more to motivate myself. Some days I feel I want to simply chill out and not do a thing. At times, I do need to take time out. I accept that is what being human is — whether you are an ex-drug user, housewife or bank manager. Being human is highs and lows, but understanding energy is a tool to stay on top — a way to stay balanced overall. It's a way to not get caught up in the mind's chatter. It's allowed me to see where I have come from and how far, given no chance by doctors of achieving healing by myself. It's allowed me to say again and again, 'I feel great today.'

I recognise and accept that I have a strong negative past. I need to honour the work I have done and not flirt with the old ways, or those channels can and will reconnect. I need to continually remain on guard for negative influences and keep on training with the higher vibrational frequency. I need *that* type of medicine, every day. My past will always be there in the background, waiting for me to slip to the old resonance. The tests will never cease. But I worked hard to enter this new space and I intend to honour it, and it will continue to protect me.

Is it the road for others? To detox, exercise or simply quit all drugs and attachment is a good start, but awareness is the key — awareness of one's body, environment and universe. This means awareness on a heart and soul level, not a body and mind level. We must raise our vibration, because in doing so, true awareness is then available. And as I have found, we must process the negative inside. My way may not be the way for some, but that is our gift of free will. For me, the aim in life is to live happy and healthy, to walk in peace, walk in friendship and walk in love... and to die with a smile. And I feel blessed that I have found a way to achieve that, especially given my past.

I once thought that healing or feeling good is a final goal or a date to aim for — 'A job well done!' Now I know that it's an obligation to honour every single day of my life. Healing my past has been the greatest challenge and the greatest achievement. But coming this far isn't the finale. Feeling good is working and staying disciplined continually. The *finale* is to ultimately live from my heart. I thought I had tasted the real thing on ecstasy, but if you've read this far, well...

At times, I reminisce that moment in the doctor's suite and his final words to me: 'If you don't take this medication, your life will not — and may never — get any better.' End quote! There's a special feeling you get when you achieve something in life you're not meant to, but you always knew you could.

I hope that this book becomes the seed that resonates with you, so you can believe it's possible to begin your own journey of change.

Do you wanna get high like you've never been before?

Yours with health, happiness and love — and a higher resonant life.

Since the author's introduction to the community of Ratu Bagus, it has grown significantly to the point of being a recognised and established alternative healing facility in both Indonesia and internationally.

If you would like more information on Ratu Bagus and his ashram, please visit:
ratubagus.com

If you would like to contact the author, please visit:
sexdrugsandtechnothebook.com

Author Bio

PAUL ELDRIDGE grew up in beachside Maroubra, Sydney, a suburb renowned for its hard-core surfing and partying lifestyle. In his late twenties, he began DJing at the leading clubs and bars around Oxford Street, in Sydney's 24/7 party strip. From that iconic dance party hub, Hordern Pavilion, to residencies at venues such as Stonewall and the Beresford, and frequent gigs along Oxford Street's bars and clubs, his venues, his music style and the crowd he attracted were usually underground and predominantly gay (though, for the record, he himself is not). In 1995 he also began the infamous long weekend recovery parties in the Beresford Hotel laneway, and presided over them for five years.

Beyond Sydney, Paul played the east coast of Australia, from Melbourne up to Townsville, and hosted music broadcasts on numerous radio stations along the way. For six years he was the resident (European) summer and New Year DJ at Double Six nightclub on Bali, and he also played at some of the island's leading dance parties, such as Ngyang Ngyang and Castaway (voted the number-one party in Southeast Asia for three consecutive years), as well as other Indonesian venues.

He now lives a very different life in Bali.

BOOKS

O is a symbol of the world, of oneness and unity. In different cultures it also means the "eye," symbolizing knowledge and insight. We aim to publish books that are accessible, constructive and that challenge accepted opinion, both that of academia and the "moral majority."

Our books are available in all good English language bookstores worldwide. If you don't see the book on the shelves ask the bookstore to order it for you, quoting the ISBN number and title. Alternatively you can order online (all major online retail sites carry our titles) or contact the distributor in the relevant country, listed on the copyright page.

See our website **www.o-books.net** for a full list of over 500 titles, growing by 100 a year.

And tune in to myspiritradio.com for our book review radio show, hosted by June-Elleni Laine, where you can listen to the authors discussing their books.

MySpiritRadio